WEIRD MOMENTS IN CLEVELAND LAND SPORTS

Bottlegate, Bedbugs, and
Burying the Pennant
and More!

Vince Guerrieri

GRAY & COMPANY, PUBLISHERS
CLEVELAND

Gray & Company, Publishers
www.grayco.com

ISBN 978-1-59851-123-9
Printed in the United States of America
1

CONTENTS

For Sammy

"ONLY IN CLEVELAND."

It's the lament of a sports fan in Northeast Ohio after every season that falls short of expectations or trade that doesn't pan out: "Only in Cleveland." If you've heard it once, you've heard it a million times, from dejected fans trudging back to the Muni Lot after a Browns loss, callers to local talk radio or fans commiserating at a bar or party.

Sure, any team's history includes hard-luck losses and bad personnel moves. For example, few would remember Giants quarterback Joe Pisarcik were it not for his fumble in the waning seconds of a game against the Eagles, leading to Herman Edwards' recovery and the "Miracle at the Meadowlands." Sacramento Kings fans still feel like the deck was stacked against them in the 2002 Western Conference Finals against the Lakers. And Cincinnati Reds fans still shake their heads at the idea of trading Frank Robinson, "an old 30," to the Orioles.

But you have to admit, a *lot* of strange things have happened in Cleveland sports. Part of that, no doubt, is because of the city's duration as home to sports teams (121 years and counting for the current baseball team, and decades before for previous iterations; 52 and counting for the current basketball team; and 76 years—with a three-year intermission—for the football team). Yet there are plenty of other cities with even more sports teams or even longer histories that can't claim the vast number of weird, random, wild, bizarre, creepy, and odd occurrences Cleveland can.

Cleveland sports teams have set records for futility in baseball, football and basketball. The last team in any of the four major leagues to fold was from Cleveland. The city's teams have had what seem to be an outsized share of front office ineptitude, absurd losses and bizarre injuries.

This book is by no means an exhaustive record of all those instances (mostly because I know six months from now, something will occur to me that I should have included). It's supposed to be a fun recounting of events that could be less than fun. Because if you can't laugh, what can you do?

ON-FIELD ABSURDITY

One of the great joys of watching sports is that there's always a chance you will see something you've never seen before. Between the lines, they say, anything can happen.

Sometimes, it's dramatic. No-hitters. Last-second Hail Mary touchdowns. Virtuoso performances from the finest athletes on the planet—and occasionally a journeyman who rises to the occasion for a piece of immortality.

And sometimes, it's just hilarious . . .

WRONG-WAY BASKET, PART I

The Cavs' first season, 1970-71, was a memorable one—for all the wrong reasons. The team began its existence with 15 straight losses. After their first win (a New York newspaper actually had a daily counter for when the Cavs would win their first game), they lost another 12. But one play against the Portland Trail Blazers—another expansion team—on Dec. 9 seemed to sum up the season's ineptitude.

Down three after three periods, Bobby Lewis recovered the jump ball that started the fourth quarter and fired a pass to John Warren. The team executed a perfect fast break, and Warren went in and laid it up before Portland's LeRoy Ellis could block the shot. It was just the way for the Cavs to start the period—"a total team effort," Warren recalled in a 2015 interview with the author. But the referee blew his whistle. Warren was afraid it was a traveling call. But the Cavs had scored in the wrong basket, and they went on to lose 109-102 to drop to 2-28.

Coach Bill Fitch was reviewing game film with the team at the next day's practice. "Bingo [Smith] was really riding John," he recalled in 2015. That stopped once they saw the play on film—with Bingo in the corner jumping up and down shouting for the ball! "As soon as I showed it, Bingo didn't say boo after that. Nobody let him forget it."

FRANK ROBINSON GETS IN A FIGHT AT A FRIENDLY

Because of contractual obligations, the Indians had a choice in 1976: They could pay their Triple-A farm team, the Toledo Mud Hens, $5,000 or play them in an exhibition game. The Indians were in dire financial straits—allegedly finishing that season $500,000 in the red—so the payment was not an option.

So the Indians took the bus ride to Maumee, Ohio and Ned Skeldon Stadium, a former racetrack that had been reconditioned into the Mud Hens' home, for the June 30 exhibition. It was a miserable night, including a 40-minute rain delay, but there were some bright spots. Coach Jeff Torborg got into the game, as did hitting coach Rocky Colavito, who was a fan favorite throughout the region, thanks to his playing career in Cleveland and Detroit.

Even player-manager Frank Robinson got into the game, inserting himself as a pinch-hitter. He stepped in, and the first pitch sailed over his head—an ostensible warning shot.

The pitcher was "Bullet" Bob Reynolds, who had been cut from the team in spring training. Worse yet, he had found out that he was cut not from Robinson or the coaching staff, but from reporters covering the team. He'd borne a grudge against Robinson since then, and now had the opportunity to share his feelings.

Robinson, always known for his competitiveness, was willing to give it right back. He flied out to center field, and according to multiple newspaper accounts, on his way back to the dugout, yelled at Reynolds, "You're gutless! If you're going to throw at someone, at least come close enough to knock him down."

"At least you're talking to me now," Reynolds replied, and the fight was on. Before Reynolds could even get his glove off, Robinson had laid him out with a left to the jaw, followed by a quick right cross. The next day's *Toledo Blade* said the fight happened so quickly that it didn't even give the dugouts a chance to empty.

Robinson was thrown out of the game. Reynolds was treated for a cut tongue and a swollen jaw. Two days later, Robinson remained defiant as he met with the media, saying he didn't have to apologize for his actions. "He's the one who started it all," Robinson said of Reynolds. "He took the cheap shot, trying to look big to his teammates."

THE STRAT-O-MATIC ALL-STAR GAME

No city warmed to a major league all-star game quite like Cleveland. Municipal Stadium had hosted three—the third-ever all-star game, in 1935; a barnburner in 1954; and the outlier in 1963 that drew small crowds and little interest—and was on pace to host a fourth in 1981 when the players went out on strike in May of that year. The strike put the Midsummer Classic, and indeed the remainder of the season, in jeopardy. Yet on the scheduled date, July 14, 1981 the All-Star Game was played at Cleveland Stadium.

Well . . . *an* All-Star Game was played.

Rocco Scotti sang the national anthem, accompanied by an accordionist. (*Sports Illustrated* said it was "the first All-Star Game that sounded like an Italian wedding.") The Indians' short-lived mascot the Baseball Bug entertained spectators. And Bob Feller came out to the roar of a crowd of 58, not to throw a ceremonial first pitch, but to throw the ceremonial first dice.

Tables were set up on the infield, where two producers from

WKYC-TV, Jim Schaefer and Jon Halpern, were playing Strat-O-Matic Baseball—a tabletop game based on real MLB players and teams—with all-star rosters from the American and National leagues.

The National League had been riding a winning streak in recent years, and that continued with the simulated game, in which they trounced the American League 15-2. Dave Parker was named the game MVP. Because there were no major sporting events going on at that point, the Strat-o-Matic game got no end of news coverage, with write-ups in local papers and on the wire, and stories on the TV news. Later that year, Schaefer and Halpern were invited to bring the board, cards and dice they had used for the game up to Cooperstown for display at the Baseball Hall of Fame.

The players' strike ended, and the real All-Star game was played on Aug. 9—the first game back for Major League Baseball. It remains the highest-attended MLB All-Star Game, as 72,086 fans—including Vice President George H.W. Bush and entertainer Bob Hope—watched the National League prevail on the field as they had recently done on the tabletop. This time, Expos catcher Gary Carter, who homered twice in the game, was the MVP.

He'd also homered in the Strat-o-Matic game. Sometimes life imitates art.

JULIO FRANCO GOES MIA

On April 19, 1985, the Indians started a three-game series against the Yankees in the Bronx. Unawed by the mystique of Yankee Stadium, the Indians beat the Bombers 2-1. Neal Heaton mowed down batters, and Julio Franco hit a two-run home run off Ron Guidry to account for the Tribe's offense.

And then Franco disappeared into the night. He was nowhere to be found before the second game of the series.

Franco was one of the Indians' more eccentric players. In 1984, before spring training, he spent two weeks in jail in his native Dominican Republic for gun possession. (He said his brother visited and hit him grounders to keep him in playing shape.) But he'd never even been so much as late for a game, manager Pat Corrales noted.

This was a time when New York City was regarded as especially dangerous. Movies like *The Warriors* and *Taxi Driver* had painted a terrifying portrait of a burnt-out, crime-infested city where just going outside seemed to take on an element of risk. Drugs were a concern within Major League Baseball. (The season would end with federal trials in Pittsburgh alleging widespread cocaine use among players.) But Franco was regarded as a gym rat who was very careful with what he ingested.

"Until I see him, I'm concerned," Corrales told the *Plain Dealer* at the time.

After the second game, a 5-2 Indians loss, Franco's teammate Tony Bernazard and hitting coach Bobby Bonds ventured out into the Bronx. They eventually found Franco at a friend's house. The story, pieced together from Franco's friends (Franco and the team officially declined comment), was that Franco went to see his friends, Juan and Marciano Todman, with whom he'd grown up in the Dominican Republic, after Friday's game. He spent the night there, and was ill the next day and slept through the game. (Marciano Todman didn't have a home phone, so there was ostensibly no way to contact the team.) Bonds and Bernazard escorted Franco back to the team's hotel in Manhattan.

Franco was fined a game's pay but was back in the lineup the next day. ("You do not penalize the ballclub, you penalize the individual," Corrales said.) His eye, though bloodshot after what writers surmised was an evening of partying, was true, as he singled in his first at-bat as the Tribe won the series with a 3-0 victory.

Franco didn't suffer any long-term effects, either. Known for his durability, he played 23 years in the major leagues, along with stints in Japan, Korea and Mexico, playing until he was 48.

A HOMER OFF JOSE'S HEAD

Rangers pitcher Kenny Rogers was staked to a three-run lead in a game against the Indians at Cleveland Stadium on May 26, 1993. It was the venerable venue's final year as the home of the Tribe, who were headed toward a sixth-place finish in the American League East.

But that day, they weren't dead and buried. In fact, they found a way to get . . . a head. (That's the limit for noggin-related puns—unlike the next day's game coverage in the *Plain Dealer*. Paul Hoynes just couldn't resist.)

Carlos Martinez led off the bottom of the fourth with the Indians down 3-1. He hit a shot to right field. He said after the game that at first he thought it would clear the fence. Then he saw outfielder Jose Canseco closing in on it and thought it would be caught.

At the warning track, the ball hit Canseco on the head. Everyone in the ballpark was looking for the ball on the ground, but Indians manager Mike Hargrove saw it glance off Canseco's head over the fence for a home run.

"You've got to laugh at something like that," Martinez said after the game, according to the *Plain Dealer*. "It's kind of funny, but that's the way this game is."

Even Canseco saw the humor in it. "I'll be on ESPN for a month," he said. (He also got mocked by David Letterman, who compiled a list of the Top Ten Things Worse Than Having a Fly Ball Bounce Off Your Head for a Home Run.)

About the only person who didn't see the humor in it was Rogers, who was barely hanging on to a spot in the Rangers' starting rotation. But he recovered enough to get his own slice of immortality: The following season he pitched a perfect game.

Canseco's error-filled day wasn't over after Martinez's homer. In the sixth inning, Carlos Baerga—who turned out to be the last batter Rogers faced that day—hit a ball to right field. Canseco was playing near the foul pole but overran the ball. He was able to get part of his glove on the ball, but it got past him for a triple. Hargrove turned the game over to the bullpen, which held on for a 7-6 win. (The Indians' winning pitcher that game? Jose Mesa, who was still a starter at that point.) To add insult to injury, Canseco went hitless in three at-bats.

"The only hit I got in the game went off my head and over the fence," he said afterward.

BOTTLEGATE

It was a Sunday in December on the lakefront in 2001. On the field in Browns Stadium, the Browns were driving, hoping for a comeback in the waning moments of a game against the Jaguars, who were already mathematically eliminated from the postseason. The Browns were 6-6, and needed a win to keep slim playoff hopes alive under first-year coach Butch Davis.

Down 15-10 late in the fourth quarter, the Browns were facing fourth and 2 from the Jaguars' 12-yard line. Tim Couch found receiver Quincy Morgan for what referees initially signaled as a completed catch for a three-yard gain and a first down.

On the next play, with less than a minute to play, Couch spiked the ball to stop the clock with 48 seconds left. The referees huddled . . . and then said Couch's fourth-down completion to Morgan was under review. NFL rules, then as now, say that any review of a play must come before the following play. Crew chief Terry McAuley, in his first season as a referee and fourth as an NFL official, said that a communication error had kept the news from being relayed before the ball was snapped.

After review, Couch's pass was ruled incomplete. The Browns had turned the ball over on downs and had no time outs. The game was effectively over, and the Jaguars would win.

Of course, some fans in the stands had a real problem with this. They voiced their opinion by showering the field not just with boos, but with debris. The game would soon become known as the Bottlegate game because of the massive amounts of plastic beer bottles—some not completely empty—thrown on to the field. "We feared for our lives," Jaguars wide receiver Jimmy Smith said, according to the Associated Press. "It was like dodging bullets."

McAuley took the unprecedented step to declare the game over with 48 seconds left, and ordered both teams off the field.

Teams were starting to undress and shower in the locker room when they were informed that the league office had called to ensure that the final, meaningless 48 seconds were played. Both teams returned to the field as Jaguars quarterback Mark Brunell took a knee on two plays to end the game.

National reaction was swift and negative.

"Cleveland Browns fans should be embarrassed today," radio host Jim Rome said, according to the *Plain Dealer*.

"Football fans in Cleveland gathered early for the traditional exchange of their favorite yuletide gifts, half-drunken bottles of beer," wrote Mike Penner of the *Los Angeles Times*.

"Now we know why they desperately wanted to have an NFL team back in town," wrote Jim McCabe of the *Boston Globe*. "They needed the big arena to showcase their bottle-tossing talents just in case it becomes an Olympic sport."

Browns President Carmen Policy, a bottle-half-full kind of guy, took the ending as a positive. "I like the fact that our fans care," he said, according to the Associated Press.

NFL Commissioner Paul Tagliabue announced following the season that the review process would itself be reviewed to avoid situations like that in the future. But the most immediate change came the following week, when alcohol sales at all NFL stadiums ended following the end of the third quarter—and the Browns stopped selling beer in bottles.

The legend of Bottlegate lives on—and not just for Browns fans. A Saints fan who filed suit against the NFL in 2018 cited Tagliabue's actions to ensure the game's final 48 seconds were played as examples of the commissioner's power—which, they argued, extended to being able to replay the end of the 2018 NFC Championship Game. In that game, a missed pass interference call against Nickell Robey-Coleman led to the Rams getting the ball back and scoring to tie the game in the final possession of regulation. They went on to win in overtime.

Of course, the Browns and Saints have a special kinship because of Bottlegate. The day after the Browns-Jaguars game in 2001, the Saints were playing on Monday night. A dubious pass interference call against New Orleans prompted the bottles to start flying at the Superdome. The Saints' opponent that week? The Rams.

THROWING AWAY A HELMET—AND A GAME

Expectations were high for the Browns in 2002. The team had gone 7-9 in 2001—more wins that season than in the previous two combined—and the playoffs were within reach.

The Browns started the season against the Chiefs. Unlike the Bottlegate game against the Jaguars, the opener in Cleveland ended with just one unnecessarily thrown projectile. But it cost the Browns the game.

The Browns were leading 30-17 early in the fourth quarter. But the Chiefs, led by running back Priest Holmes, battled back to pull within two, 39-37. With four seconds left in the game, it looked like the Browns might escape with the win as Chiefs' quarterback Trent Green dropped back to pass and the Browns defense brought everything but the proverbial kitchen sink. Linebacker Dwayne Rudd brought down Green, saw triple zeroes on the game clock and, exulting in what he thought was a hard-fought win, ripped off his helmet and flung it in triumph.

The only problem was that the game wasn't over. Before going down, Green had lateraled the ball to lineman John Tait, who then lumbered 28 yards down the sideline to the Browns' 25. But time had run out, so it was a moot point, right? Not exactly.

Rudd's helmet toss had garnered a 15-yard unsportsmanlike conduct penalty. And an NFL game can't end on a defensive penalty—a rule that Browns fans are probably more acutely aware of than any other fan base. Tack on the half-the-distance-to-the-goal yards, and kicker Morten Andersen had a virtual chip shot. He made the 30-yard field goal, and the Chiefs snatched victory from the jaws of defeat.

"I thought we had won," Rudd told the media after the game.

WRONG-WAY BASKET, PART II

Occasionally, history repeats itself. Take, for instance, the Cavs-Jazz game of March 16, 2003. The Cavs, at that point, were dreadful, ultimately bottoming out that season with 17 wins.

But on this particular afternoon, they were winning and held an almost insurmountable lead against Utah in the final seconds of the game, thanks in no small part to the efforts of Ricky Davis, who led all scorers with 26 points and had dished out 12 assists and pulled down nine rebounds. That left him one shy of a triple-double. So Davis tried to take matters into his own hands. He took the inbounds pass, and was supposed to dribble to run out the clock to secure the win for the Cavs—just their second win in 15 games. Instead, Davis turned toward the Cavs' own basket and lofted a "shot" to hit the rim. He pulled the ball down, confident that he'd gotten his 10th rebound for the triple-double.

The Jazz's DeShawn Stevenson, upset—rightly—at Davis' attempt to show them up, fouled him hard. Davis hit two free throws to finish the game with 28 points, but the triple-double eluded him. (It's against the rules to shoot at your own basket, so Davis wasn't credited with a rebound.) What didn't elude him, however, was universal scorn. The wrong-way basket by the Cavs back in their first season had been a charming example of an expansion team's ineptitude. Davis' actions, on the other hand, were in service of padding his own stat line.

"DeShawn fouled him, and I would have fouled him, too," Jazz coach Jerry Sloan said in a news conference after the game. "I would have knocked him on his ass."

"They should be mad," Davis said, according to the Associated Press. "Any team that gets beat that bad shouldn't be happy. But I wouldn't do it again."

In a column for ESPN.com, David Aldridge called it "a whole new level of bush previously undiscovered by the world's top archaeologists." Aldridge pointed out that there were allegations that the Cavs were tanking to get the top overall pick in the hopes of drafting LeBron James, and Davis' actions—even during a rare win—were just another example of how inept the team was.

A chastened Davis was fined an undisclosed amount by the team for unsportsmanlike conduct. But a new nickname was born: Wrong Way Ricky.

After the season, the Cavs landed the first overall pick in the NBA draft, which they used on LeBron James—a move that thrilled Davis. "I thought LeBron James was just going to be another addition to help me score," he said, a quote that lives on in infamy.

The Cavs dealt Davis 22 games into LeBron's time in Cleveland.

ATTACK OF THE MIDGES

In 2007, for the first time in six years, the Indians won the American League Central Division. The team had a new crop of stars, including a rotation anchored by eventual Cy Young Award winner CC Sabathia and the pitcher then known as Fausto Carmona. Fan favorite Grady Sizemore patrolled centerfield, the batting lineup featured power hitters like Travis Hafner and Victor Martinez, and rookie infielder Asdrubal Cabrera showed a tantalizing glimpse of things to come. Even Kenny Lofton, then in the nomadic phase of his career, had rejoined the Indians, a reminder of those juggernaut teams that had won five straight division titles in the 1990s.

The Indians finished the season one game behind the AL East

Division champion Red Sox, who had the best record in the majors. Rules in place at the time kept the top seed—Boston—from playing the wild card team if they were from the same division, which was the case that year. So the Red Sox would play the West Division champs, the Angels, and the Indians would meet a familiar foe, the Yankees.

Just as the Indians were revitalized in the 1990s, the Yankees had once again risen to prominence and were every bit the dynasty in the AL East that the Indians were in the Central, with one glaring difference: The Yankees went to four straight World Series (and five in six years), winning all but one. The Indians made two World Series appearances, losing both. (When it comes to baseball in Cleveland, there's no hate like Yankees hate.)

The first two games of the best-of-five series were in Cleveland. The Indians cruised to a 12-3 win in Game 1. The next game was tighter. The Yankees' Melky Cabrera hit a solo home run in the third inning for the first run of the game, and the score remained 1-0. With one out in the bottom of the seventh, shortstop Jhonny Peralta doubled and Lofton walked. Yankees pitcher Andy Pettitte was lifted for Joba Chamberlain, the highly touted reliever who'd come up to the majors just two months earlier. He put out the fire by fanning Franklin Gutierrez and inducing Casey Blake to ground out.

And then the midges came.

Anyone who's grown up near Lake Erie knows that midges are an unwelcome but not particularly dangerous fact of life from late spring through late summer. Actually, a large midge population is a good sign for the health of the lake and its ecosystem. But they're attracted to warm temperatures and bright lights—both available in abundance for the game, which had a first-pitch temperature of 81 degrees at 5:09 p.m.

In the bottom of the eighth, the midges descended upon Chamberlain, swarming around him and coming to rest on him, literally covering the back of his neck. The pitcher was rattled. He walked Sizemore on four straight pitches, and then threw a wild pitch that allowed him to take second. Sizemore advanced to third on a sacrifice by Asdrubal Cabrera, and then Chamberlain uncorked his second wild pitch of the inning, allowing Sizemore to race home to score the tying run. Chamberlain had thrown just one wild pitch during the entire regular season.

In the top of the ninth inning, Tribe pitcher Fausto Carmona was straight up dealing, cool, calm and collected. "Just when you think you've seen it all—bugs," Derek Jeter told the *New York Times*. "That's home-field advantage."

Chamberlain was lifted in the bottom of the ninth for Yankees closer Mariano Rivera. The game went into extra innings tied at 1. In the bottom of the 10th, the Tribe loaded the bases but couldn't push the winning run across. They loaded the bases again in the 11th, and this time, Hafner delivered, lacing a line drive single to center field for the win.

Later, Yankees manager Joe Torre said his biggest regret was not pulling his team from the field when the midges descended. In the middle of the eighth, Yankees trainer Gene Monahan had come out to spray Chamberlain with bug spray—as it turns out, the exact wrong thing to do. (Insect repellent doesn't work on midges, and in fact, attracts them. "Vinegar or dryer sheets," Chamberlain told MLB.com ruefully a decade later.)

The series moved on to the Bronx, where the Yankees won Game 3 before the Indians took Game 4 and the series. Chamberlain's career was relatively brief and unspectacular, given the hype that had preceded him. He actually ended his career with the Indians. Although he has since talked at length about the midge game, he told the *New York Post* on the game's ten-year anniversary that he could never watch it in its entirety.

PHIL DAWSON'S GOOSENECK KICK

Since the Browns' return in 1999, not a lot has gone the team's way. But one Sunday afternoon in Baltimore, the ball bounced their way—literally.

With 3:42 left in the third quarter against the Ravens on Nov. 18, 2007, the Browns were leading 27-14, thanks to a 100-yard interception return by Browns safety Brodney Pool for a touchdown to thwart a potential game-tying drive by the Ravens. But Baltimore started chipping away, thanks to kicker Matt Stover—the sole remaining Ravens player who had been part of the team when it moved from Cleveland. He booted a pair of field goals to pull the Ravens within a score, and Ravens quarterback Kyle Boller led a three-play, no-huddle drive that culminated in a 27-yard touchdown pass to tie the game with 3:31 left. The Browns punted on the ensuing possession, the Ravens took over, and Stover booted the go-ahead field goal with 26 seconds left.

The Ravens had scored 16 straight points, and Browns fans everywhere were mumbling about their bad fortune.

But the Browns had one last chance to tie the game. On the final play of the game, Phil Dawson lined up for a 51-yard field goal attempt. Even for the sure-footed kicker, it was far from a sure thing. He'd already missed one field goal this game, and the week before had come up short on a 52-yard attempt into the open end zone at Heinz Field in Pittsburgh, trying to send that game to overtime.

Against the Ravens, Dawson booted the ball, which hooked to the left and hit the upright . . . and then appeared to bounce off the crossbar back onto the field in front of the goal posts. Field Judge Jim Saracino waved the kick no good, and the Ravens celebrated a come-from-behind division win that kept their playoff hopes alive. Both teams knelt at midfield for a postgame prayer, then went into their locker rooms.

Browns head coach Romeo Crennel couldn't challenge the play. Then as now, any review in the last two minutes of the game can come only from the booth. Yet no official replay could happen, either: Field goals weren't reviewable plays. The play had slipped into a netherworld of NFL officiating, and the officials were conferring.

Dawson thought maybe the kick had been good.

"I couldn't tell for sure. I could tell by the way it glanced off the upright, it looked like it went forward," he told media after the game. "But we had people down near the goal post who were screaming at the top of their lungs that it had hit whatever that bar you call it."

After five minutes or so of "conference"—referee Pete Morelli took pains not to say the play was "reviewed"— Morelli announced that the field goal had hit the gooseneck portion of the goal post, on the far side of the uprights, and the kick was good.

The teams had to be taken out of the locker rooms to play overtime.

The Browns won the coin toss, and then engineered a brief drive to culminate in a 31-yard field goal attempt by Dawson. This one was good without a doubt, and the Browns won, sweeping the season series against the Ravens for the first time since 2001.

"This is a first," Dawson said, in a story by Cleveland.com's Mary Kay Cabot. "I wish I had something profound to say. I'm a little numb. We went from the high of highs to the low of lows and right back to the mountaintop."

The Ravens were stunned. They'd seemingly snatched victory from the jaws of defeat—only to have it snatched away from them.

"It was just weird," Ravens receiver Derrick Mason said, according to the *Baltimore Sun*. "Just when you thought everything that had gone wrong you had overcome it, then there's another thing. They probably made the right call."

BRANDON WEEDEN AND THE
RED, WHITE AND BLUE

In what seemed to be an annual occurrence, the Browns drafted yet another quarterback in 2012. They were in dire need of a change from Colt McCoy. The 2011 Browns had been one of the worst offensive teams in the league.

Like in 2007, when they picked Brady Quinn, the Browns used the 22nd pick in the first round to take a quarterback, Brandon Weeden. It was an odd choice, even by Browns standards. Weeden was 28 years old. He'd washed out of minor league baseball after being drafted by the Yankees, then went to Oklahoma State, where he threw for more than 4,000 yards in back-to-back years—after walking on to the team.

Browns President Mike Holmgren, who had never drafted a quarterback in the first round in his lengthy and to that point successful career as an NFL coach and executive, had been willing to trade up for one of the two quarterbacks that were the consensus best in that draft: Stanford's Andrew Luck or Baylor's Robert Griffin III. But the Colts—hurting from Peyton Manning appearing to reach the end of the line—took Luck first overall. The Rams had the second pick—and many suitors trying to trade for it. The Browns were among them, but the Rams made the deal with Washington, which took Griffin.

The next quarterback off the board was Ryan Tannehill, taken eighth overall by the Dolphins. Then the Browns took Weeden with a pick they'd gotten from Atlanta the year before.

"When we went through the process of evaluating him, we became very fond of him," coach Pat Shurmur said in a news conference after the first round. "We all did. From [owner] Randy [Lerner] to [president] Mike [Holmgren] to [GM] Tom [Heckert] to myself. We came away saying, 'This is a guy we'd like to have on our team.'"

There was no doubt that Weeden would be the Browns' starter

as the season began. And that was the plan on Sept. 9, 2012, when Weeden would start for the Browns in their season opener against the Eagles.

Weeden was on the field during warm-ups, throwing the football, when as part of the pregame preparations, a group of U.S. service members started unfurling a huge American flag in Weeden's path. "Got no warning," Weeden told Yahoo Sports reporter Mike Silver in a text that night. "Was throwing like I always do and they came haulin' ass with that thing right at me." Weeden, showing the type of situational awareness that was a hallmark of his Browns career, ducked under the flag, eventually emerging on the other side. He hoped his teammates hadn't noticed. But the TV viewing audience saw.

Weeden then went on to play one of the worst games in NFL history, going 12-for-35 passing, for 118 yards. Despite that, the Browns were still in the game, and had a chance to win with a last-minute drive—until Weeden threw his fourth interception of the game, which he finished with an astonishing 5.1 quarterback rating.

"Maybe he should have stayed under the flag," Cindy Boren wrote in the *Washington Post* the next day.

Weeden was released after two seasons, in which he threw more interceptions (26) than touchdowns (23). The Browns would then draft . . . Johnny Manziel, also with the 22nd overall pick. And the circle of life continued.

Weeden's career was bad even by Browns standards, but the 2012 draft class was a strange one for quarterbacks: The late rounds yielded some good finds, while the highest-drafted QBs amounted to little.

Nick Foles, taken in the third round (88th overall pick), stepped in as Eagles quarterback and led them to a Super Bowl win. Kirk Cousins, ostensibly drafted in the fourth round (102nd overall) to back up Griffin in Washington, went on to have a decent career. And the most successful quarterback from that draft was Russell Wilson, who'd distinguished himself at Wisconsin following a brief foray in the Colorado Rockies system. Wilson was drafted in the third round (75th overall) by the Seahawks. (Of course there were two former minor league baseball players turned quarterbacks in the draft that year—and the Browns took the wrong one.)

The highest-drafted ones amounted to little. Plagued by injuries, Luck retired after seven seasons. Injuries also shortened Griffin's career. Ryan Tannehill was able to resurrect his career after leaving Miami for Tennessee. Brock Osweiler, taken in the second round by the Broncos, spent seven years in the NFL with four different teams—including the Browns, who took him as part of a salary dump by his former team, the Houston Texans.

After his rookie year, Weeden never started more than five games in a season again, and he was soon out of the league. The quarterback he was drafted to replace, Colt McCoy, has maintained an active NFL career as a backup, with an occasional spot start. Of course, he's three years younger than Weeden.

"BAD BOWL" LOSS TO THE LIONS

In the 1950s, the Lions and Browns were two of the best teams in the NFL, meeting regularly in the NFL Championship Game.

When the Browns returned as an expansion team, there were attempts to gin up a rivalry between the two teams with an annual preseason game, grandiosely called the Great Lakes Classic. (There was even a trophy with a barge on it, symbolizing the Great Lakes but looking to more than one person like the ill-fated Edmund Fitzgerald.) In the 2000s, the Browns and Lions were the dregs of the NFL. The Browns were an expansion team that seemed unable even a decade later to find their footing, and the Lions had suffered the ignominy of the first 0-16 season in NFL history in 2008.

The following year, the Browns and Lions met in a regular season game in November. Each had one win at the time. The Lions were thrilled, because it was already one more than they'd had the previous season. But for the Browns, it was an ominous start for new coach Eric Mangini.

The Browns appeared headed for a win, with a 37-31 lead after the two-minute warning. But on a play that could have potentially sealed the game, quarterback Brady Quinn threw an incompletion to Mohamed Massaquoi on third and five, and the Browns punted the ball away. Rookie quarterback Matthew Stafford had 1:42 to win the game.

Stafford led the Lions to the Browns' 32. On what appeared to be the final play of the game, from the 32-yard line, he threw a pass that was intercepted by Brodney Pool in the end zone. But Hank Poteat had been whistled for defensive pass interference, and as Browns fans learned bitterly against Kansas City in 2002, the game can't end on a defensive penalty.

Stafford was hurting from what appeared to be a dislocated shoulder after C.J. Mosley tackled him and landed on him, and it looked like Daunte Culpepper would have to relieve him at quarterback. But Mangini called a time out to get the defense to regroup— and Stafford regrouped as well, running in for the game's final play. This time, from the one-yard line, he found Brandon Pettigrew for a touchdown to tie the game. Jason Hanson kicked the extra point, and the Lions snapped their six-game losing streak. (The Browns' was at five and counting.)

"I'm just sick with the way this thing ended," Mangini said, according to Tony Grossi, who was covering the game for the *Plain Dealer*. Grossi said at the time that it was the strangest ending ever to a Browns game.

That proclamation tempted fate. Things would get much stranger.

KICK-SIX AGAINST THE RAVENS

The Browns were hosting the Ravens for a Monday night game in 2015. Once upon a time, a Monday night game made the whole city stop and take notice, but the reaction was tepid for this one. The Browns had lost five games in a row. The Ravens were going nowhere fast as well, at 3-7 only a win better than the Browns. The game was a matchup of two journeyman quarterbacks. Josh McCown would get the start for the Browns, with Austin Davis serving as his backup. Ravens quarterback Joe Flacco was out due to injury, so Matt Schaub was the starting quarterback instead.

Injuries had decimated Baltimore, and it seemed like the kind of game where the Browns could snap their losing skid. And in the game's waning moments, it appeared that would happen. Davis had come in to replace McCown, who went out with a shoulder injury with less than two minutes to play, and he hit Travis Benjamin for a touchdown to tie the game at 27.

With 50 seconds left, the Browns got the ball back on a Schaub interception, and the Browns could kick a potential 51-yard field goal to win the game.

It wasn't a chip shot, but the night was clear and Travis Coons had made all 18 kicks he'd attempted that season. Coons made what he called a good kick for what was poised to be the game-winning field goal. But defensive end Brent Urban, playing his first NFL game, was able to get a hand on it. Will Hill scooped up the ball and returned it 64 yards for a touchdown. That the Browns had lost again wasn't a surprise. But the way it happened was unique, even for fans used to losing in seemingly every way possible.

"Tough one to wrap your brain around," a taciturn coach Mike Pettine said in his news conference following the game.

Ain't that the truth.

J.R. FORGETS THE SCORE

In the 2018 NBA postseason, the Cavaliers advanced to their fourth straight NBA Finals. Once again, their opponent would be the Golden State Warriors. It was the first time in any of the four major league sports that the same teams met for the championship in four consecutive years. The Warriors were once again favored to win the series, which would start in Oakland.

But it actually looked like the Cavs would steal the first game. Down one with 4.7 seconds left to play, the Cavaliers' George Hill hit a free throw to tie the game at 107. He then clanked his second free throw, but his teammate J. R. Smith came down with the rebound.

Smith had come to the Cavs midway through the 2015 season, recognized as a talented if not always focused basketball player. He had been a vital part of the 2016 championship team, and his shirtless antics during the championship parade had endeared him to fans throughout Northeast Ohio. Now, he had a chance at heroics again. A putback basket would give the Cavs a win and potentially set the Warriors back on their heels.

Instead, he dribbled the ball, running out the clock. He said immediately afterward that he had been looking for a time out to be called for a reset, allowing the Cavs to take a last shot. But later on, after the heat of the moment had passed, he revealed that he might have thought the Cavs were leading, and he just needed to dribble out the clock.

"Players fuck up, it just so happened that mine was in the Finals," he said a year later on *All the Smoke* on Showtime. "We've all messed up."

It's easy to wonder what might have been. Would a Cavs road win in Game 1 have turned the tide in the series? Or would it just have postponed the inevitable?

The Cavs went meekly in the ensuing overtime, losing 124-114, and then went on to be swept in four games. LeBron left after the season, and eventually, so did Smith.

MYLES AND MASON

In 2019, the Browns finally appeared to have some talent and were starting to get it together. The *Sports Illustrated* NFL preview featured Browns wide receivers Jarvis Landry and Odell Beckham Jr.—a splashy acquisition from the Giants—on the cover. The Browns were a trendy pick not just to make the playoffs (for the first time since 2002), but even go to the Super Bowl!

Unfortunately, head coach Freddie Kitchens appeared to be in over his head. The Browns showed flashes of brilliance, but quarterback Baker Mayfield regressed and the team's offensive weapons seemed poorly utilized. They were 3-6 when the Steelers came to town for a Thursday night game in November.

The Steelers had lost quarterback Ben Roethlisberger to an elbow injury earlier in the season but were 5-4 and still in the thick of the playoff race. But the Browns weren't limited to a spoiler role at that point; the playoffs weren't out of reach—as long as they took care of business.

And against the Steelers, they did. The game between the two turnpike rivals was chippy, as it can often get, but the Browns were in command throughout the game and heading for their first win against Pittsburgh since 2014. But in the game's waning seconds, defensive end Myles Garrett tackled Steelers quarterback Mason Rudolph, who had been filling for the injured Roethlisberger.

What happened next is a matter of some conjecture. Rudolph pulled at Garrett's helmet, and Garrett responded in kind. Garrett maintained that Rudolph used a racial slur (no evidence was found to corroborate Garrett's account), and the defensive end lost his cool and tried to hit the quarterback with his own helmet, which had come off as the two players jawed at each other. The melee was on.

Ultimately, both teams were fined, and Garrett was suspended until further notice. Also suspended were Steelers center Maurkice Pouncey and Browns lineman Larry Ogunjobi. Garrett and

Rudolph were also fined. All told, 33 players were fined a total of more than $700,000.

The Browns won again the following week, over the Dolphins, and the playoffs still seemed within reach. They would play the Steelers at Heinz Field the next week. In that game, Mason Rudolph continued to scuffle as quarterback and was replaced by Devlin "Duck" Hodges. It was a winnable game for the Browns, who could move to .500 and remain in the hunt for a playoff spot. But after jumping out to a 10-point lead, the Browns sputtered and eventually lost, 20-13.

A couple days before the game, Kitchens went to the theater, ironically to see *A Beautiful Day in the Neighborhood*, a movie about Pittsburgh-area native Fred Rogers. After the movie, Kitchens posed for a photo with a fan who recognized him. The shirt Kitchens was wearing was a gift from his daughters. It was made by GV Artwork, one of the Cleveland-area companies that offer witty apparel as part of Northeast Ohio's T-shirt-industrial complex. It said, "Pittsburgh Started It."

The photo made its way to social media and went viral. The reaction was predictable. "I thought it was pretty stupid," Steelers offensive lineman David DeCastro said after the game, according to the *Plain Dealer*. "Of course it's going to motivate us."

Kitchens, for his part, owned his mistakes, both sartorial and game-planning. "The T-shirt didn't cause us to give up 40-yard passes," he said.

Quarterback Baker Mayfield was similarly phlegmatic. "It's just a T-shirt. I've done much worse."

KEVIN LOVE "F*#@ED UP"

By the end of the 2020–21 NBA season, Kevin Love had 1,449 career turnovers, averaging about 2 per game for his career.

One in particular will go down in infamy.

The Cavs were playing the Raptors on April 26, 2021, and with the clock ticking down in the third period, had pulled within four points after being down 10 just two minutes earlier. Malachi Flynn drove for a layup to stretch the Raptors' lead to six. Love had been driven into the basket stanchion and was annoyed that no foul had been called.

Earlier in the game, he'd been shoved, also with no call.

Love stepped out of bounds, glowering at the officials. Referee Brandon Schwab threw Love the ball for an inbounds pass. He petulantly swatted the ball, which went in bounds. Toronto's Stanley Johnson grabbed the loose ball and dished it to Flynn at the top of the arc, who hit a three-pointer to put the Raptors up nine.

On the next play, Love got whistled for a shooting foul, and Freddie Gillespie made a pair of free throws. The Cavs ended the quarter down 11, and ended up losing the game by 16.

Almost immediately following the game, Love was roundly excoriated—and deservedly so. He admitted as much during remarks to the media the following day after the team's shootaround, leading off with an honest, if not eloquent, mea culpa.

"The reality of it is I fucked up," he said.

IT SEEMED LIKE A GOOD IDEA AT THE TIME ...

A lot of moments that turn out bad started out with the kernel of a decent idea. Images of success dance in our heads. But the reality—usually on the plot of land that was first home to Cleveland Stadium and is now home to FirstEnergy Stadium—can fall far short of the ideal, and most of the time, it happens in such a fashion that the stories about it are told for years to come ...

THE GREAT LAKES BOWL

If you saw it in the last 20 or so years of its existence, it was hard to imagine Cleveland Municipal Stadium as anything other than a rotting mass of steel, brick and peeling paint held together with bird droppings on the edge of the lakeshore. Built with a capacity of more than 80,000 in the early 1930s, the Stadium was fun when it was a packed for Browns games, but for Indians games, which drew significantly smaller crowds, it felt even more cavernous than it was.

At one time, though, the Stadium symbolized what was right with Cleveland—a city of industry, innovation and potential. But even then, there was a problem: They couldn't find teams to play there.

The stadium opened in 1931 with a heavyweight fight between Max Schmeling and Young Stribling. A year later, the Indians played their first game there, a day after formally signing the lease to play full time at the stadium. But it was the throes of the Great Depression, and the Indians, like most sports teams, were struggling to keep the team on the field and the checks clearing. So after less than two years at Municipal Stadium, they returned to League Park on the east side. It was smaller, but it was paid for. In a great irony, when Municipal Stadium hosted the 1935 All-Star Game, that was the only Major League Baseball game in the stadium that year.

The Browns were still a decade away. Cleveland's NFL franchise in the late 1930s and early 1940s was the Rams, who bounced around various ballparks in the city, playing some games at Municipal Stadium, some at League Park—and at least one season at Shaw Stadium in East Cleveland. (That city was home to National Electric Lamp—later part of General Electric—and because of that, Shaw Stadium got lights before Cleveland Stadium did.) Cleveland Municipal Stadium was already on the verge of becoming a white elephant, and organizers scrambled to find any event that could be held there.

The annual Charity Game drew thousands to watch local high school football powerhouses match up. The Stadium hosted midget car racing and track meets. When the Republicans came to town for their convention in 1936, it almost served as a backdrop for Alf Landon's acceptance speech as the presidential nominee—until it was revealed that Landon wasn't even coming to Cleveland for the convention. It regularly hosted college football games—most frequently between Notre Dame and the U.S. Naval Academy—and for one brief moment, a college bowl game.

In the 1930s and 1940s, Notre Dame was one of the great powers of college football, attracting legions of what became known as "subway alumni," people in big cities like New York, Chicago and Cleveland who had never attended Notre Dame—or possibly any other college—but felt a kinship because of their Irish or Catholic background. The most powerful team of the Big Ten at the time was the University of Michigan. Therefore, when the Knights of Columbus, already sponsors of a popular track and field meet in Cleveland, decided to hold a football bowl game, they invited Michigan and Notre Dame to play in it. It was nothing shy of chutzpah, but optimism to the point of delusion was in bloom in Cleveland after World War II, as the city peaked in population and was already touting itself as the "Best Location in the Nation."

Notre Dame turned them down flat. It was nothing personal. The Irish didn't play in any bowl games between 1925 and 1970. The Big Ten had just signed its agreement to send its champion to the Rose Bowl. "In my judgment, there is no chance whatsoever of this game being played," Conference Commissioner Tug Williams told the *Plain Dealer*.

But on Dec. 6, 1947, a football bowl game was played at Cleveland Stadium—the Great Lakes Bowl, one of five new bowl games in college football that season. The participants were both Wildcats: Villanova and Kentucky. It was Villanova's second bowl game, after the Bacardi Bowl a decade earlier. (True story: That game was played in Cuba, making it the first college football game played outside of the United States—and was preceded by a coup by Fulgencio Batista. Organizers had to reprint the game's programs at Batista's, uh, request, to ensure there were pictures of him in it).

Kentucky was under the guidance of a coach who had more than a passing familiarity with the Cleveland area. Paul "Bear" Bryant had lived with his sister in Parma during summers when he was a student at the University of Alabama. He recalled spending any spare time he had at League Park watching the Indians, and claimed to have been in the stands for the 1929 game when Babe Ruth hit his 500th home run.

The Great Lakes Bowl game was played before a crowd of 15,000—small potatoes in a stadium that seated more than 80,000. By comparison, a year earlier, the annual Charity Game, between high schools Cathedral Latin and Holy Name, had drawn more than 70,000. It was estimated that 20,000 tickets were sold for the Great Lakes Bowl, but 5,000 people opted not to brave the frigid temperatures. Bryant later called it the "coldest darn place in the world." Kentucky prevailed 24-14—for Bryant's first bowl victory—after holding off a Villanova fourth-quarter rally. Organizers had deemed it successful enough to play again the following year, this time between John Carroll University (organizers believed one of the reasons so few people showed up the previous year was because there was no team of real local interest) and Canisius College, in Buffalo. John Carroll scored late for the 14-13 win in front of more than 17,000 fans.

The Great Lakes Bowl went by the wayside after that, a curiosity of a cold-weather bowl with no conference affiliation that was still able to put on a pair of entertaining games.

BURYING THE PENNANT

Bill Veeck's brief ownership of the Indians is known for many things, including the racial integration of the American League, the last World Series win to date for Cleveland and a regularly packed Municipal Stadium, with fans lured in by a talented team and Veeck's genius at promotion.

But things took a turn for the bizarre as the 1949 season drew to a close. A crowd of nearly 30,000 gathered on Sept. 23, 1949, for the last night game of the season in Cleveland. The Indians, defending World Series champions, fought gamely to the end of the season, but had been finally eliminated from the pennant race the day before. Shortly before the game's 8:30 start, a horse-drawn hearse made its way across the field at Cleveland Stadium. Atop it, in a black coat and silk hat, was Veeck. The hearse circled the field, followed by players, coaches and other team employees walking behind. Workers lowered the 14-by-20-foot pennant from the center field flagpole and placed it in a pine coffin, which was carried by pallbearers including general manager Hank Greenberg, traveling secretary Spud Goldstein, publicist Marshall Samuel, manager Lou Boudreau and coaches Bill McKechnie, Steve O'Neill and Muddy Ruel. Business Manager Rudie Schaffer, dressed as a minister wearing a frock coat and top hat, performed the service, reading from *The Sporting News*—"the Bible of Baseball." (Schaffer was regularly willing to ham it up with Veeck, portraying the drummer when Veeck recreated the "Spirit of '76" painting for the bicentennial. Schaffer was again working with Veeck, who owned the White Sox at the time.)

The pennant was then buried behind the outfield fence, with a cardboard "tombstone" reading, "Here lies the 1948 champs." The Indians, clearly in mourning, lost that night's game 5-0 to the Tigers.

The plans for the mock funeral had been scrupulously guarded by Veeck prior to the event and no advance notice had been given to fans and reporters—seemingly out of character for a man who relished promotions. *The Sporting News* said reaction among the lords of baseball—the owners, front office people, and others who ran the sport—was mixed: "Veeck's admirers point out that the mock funeral he staged . . . was a healthy indication that this hard-fighting executive, so adept at dishing it out, also knows how to take it. His critics insist that the collapse of a world championship club is something to be borne in silent sorrow." It should be noted that his critics typically included *The Sporting News*, which found his brand of promotion a little too much for the National Pastime.

The funeral also turned out to be one of Veeck's last public appearances as Indians owner. Needing cash for his impending divorce settlement, Veeck sold the team to a partnership headed by Ellis Ryan. But his adventures in sports ownership were far from over. He later bought the moribund St. Louis Browns, engaging in promotions like allowing fans to manage and bringing the 3-foot, 7-inch-tall Eddie Gaedel up to bat, and twice owned the White Sox in his hometown of Chicago.

Cleveland's 1948 pennant has never been found. Longtime Indians groundskeeper Harold Bossard was quoted in the *Plain*

Dealer in 1975 saying that it had been dug up the next day. "[Veeck] wanted the casket that had been used because he borrowed it from a funeral director, and if he didn't return it, it would have cost him a couple thousand dollars," Bossard said.

But what about the pennant? Was it lost in the move to Jacobs Field? Accidentally thrown out? Or is it in someone's rec room, an urban legend told with a knowing wink? It remains one of the great mysteries of Cleveland sports.

10-CENT BEER NIGHT

By the 1970s, thanks in large part to flamboyant owners like Bill Veeck, promotions were viewed as necessary throughout Major League Baseball. Veeck's exploding scoreboard at Comiskey Park— replete with fireworks, loud noises and flashing lights—gave rise to a variety of entertaining scoreboards using the latest technology. And teams' schedules were dotted with promotions, from bat give-aways to Ladies' Days. Some promotions went better than others. And then there was 10-Cent Beer Night at Cleveland Stadium in 1974.

The Indians had come off a miserable 1973 season, finishing 26½ games back in the American League East with a lackluster team playing in front of crowds so sparse that the Opening Day crowd of 74,420 constituted more than 10 percent of the season's total attendance. It had been 15 years since the Tribe had drawn at least a million fans in a season, and in that time, the team had been linked to multiple cities for potential relocation. Clearly, promotions were needed to keep fans interested—and that included four 10-cent beer nights sprinkled throughout the schedule.

It wasn't unprecedented. The Indians had done it before, and the Texas Rangers had been running similar promotions successfully. The promotion was self-explanatory: For 10 cents, you got a beer that normally cost 65 cents.

The Rangers would be the opponents on June 4, 1974. Some bad blood was already brewing between the two teams. A week earlier, on May 29—during one of the Rangers' own 10-cent beer nights—tempers had flared when Lenny Randle bunted and then collided with pitcher Milt Wilcox, who was covering first. Earlier in the game, Randle had slid hard into second to break up a double play. Then, when Randle next came up to bat, Wilcox had thrown at Randle in retaliation for the hard slide. After the bunt and the collision at first, a brawl ensued, with some Rangers fans throwing food and beer at Indians manager Ken Aspromonte and Indians players when they returned to the dugout. After the game, Rangers manager Billy Martin—himself no stranger to fights on or off the field—was asked if they'd get a similar reception the following week in Cleveland. "They don't have enough fans there to worry about," he said. It was a fateful prediction.

A week later, under a full moon, the Indians and Rangers met again. More than 26,000 people were in attendance at Cleveland Stadium, and it became readily apparent that most weren't there for the game. All told, it was estimated more than 65,000 beers were sold, as vendors were overwhelmed, and soon, fans were getting refills from beer trucks parked beyond the outfield. A woman flashed the umpiring crew and tried to get a kiss. Two men jumped out of the stands and mooned Rangers players. Fans were shooting off their own fireworks, heaping enough abuse on Rangers pitchers that they had to leave the bullpen and take shelter in the dugout, and running across the expansive outfield grass.

The fans were missing a great game. The Rangers stormed out to a 5-1 lead, but the Tribe cut it to 5-3, and then tied the game in the bottom of the ninth. With two on and two out, the Indians were poised to rally for the win. Then fans jumped onto the field—again—and tried to take Rangers right fielder Jeff Burroughs' hat. Burroughs fell down, and Martin, thinking Burroughs been attacked, "ordered the charge of the light brigade," as former Indians pitcher Dick Bosman recalled in a 2014 interview with the author. Aspromonte and players left their dugout to aid the

Rangers. A melee erupted, overwhelming the already stretched security forces of 50 stadium officers and two off-duty police officers. Twenty police cars responded and ultimately, umpire Nestor Chylak was forced to declare the game a forfeit, the first MLB game so declared since fans overran Robert F. Kennedy Stadium at the last Washington Senators game three years earlier. (Ironically, the Senators were then decamping from the nation's capital to the Dallas area, where they became . . . the Texas Rangers. The starting pitcher that day for Washington, in an odd coincidence, was Dick Bosman).

The Indians had three more 10-cent beer nights scheduled later in the season. You might think that after the fiasco in June, those would all be canceled. You'd be wrong. One in July actually outdrew the June promotion, with a crowd of more than 41,000. Of course, the pitching matchup likely helped: Indians ace Gaylord Perry was up against Catfish Hunter and the defending champion Athletics. The A's prevailed 3-2 before a far more docile crowd. It probably helped that less beer was available (only the first two beers were 10 cents; after that, it went to regular price) and more security was on hand. And there was no full moon.

The national reaction to the 10-cent beer riot, naturally, was one of absolute horror. It was, as *New York Times* sportswriter Dave Anderson wrote, riffing off a beer ad at the time, "the beer that made Cleveland infamous."

"They lure people into the park by offering a beer giveaway," wrote Dick Young of the *New York Daily News*, the dean of baseball writers. "So crowds go there to tank up, not to watch baseball. What do the Lords of Baseball expect?" "How utterly stupid," wrote Wayne Minshew of the *Atlanta Constitution*. "How insane. How disgusting."

But in the years since, it's taken on almost a mythical sheen. Today at Progressive Field, souvenir stands sell T-shirts with a design of the old stadium saying "10-cent beer night, June 4, 1974." They don't commemorate the one they got right.

STEPIEN'S SOFTBALL STUNT

For as long as there have been tall buildings, people have wanted to throw things off them. Sometimes, particularly daring souls have been willing to try to catch those things. In 1908, Washington Senators catcher Gabby Street caught a baseball thrown from the top of the Washington Monument. And in 1938, the Come to Cleveland Committee—in an effort to bring positive publicity to the city—organized a similar stunt. Indians third baseman Ken Keltner went to the top of the Terminal Tower—then the tallest building outside of New York City—and threw baseballs to a waiting crowd of Indians players below. (Catchers Frank Pytlak and Henry Helf each caught one.)

In 1980, during a series of celebrations commemorating the tower's 50th anniversary, the stunt was performed again—with fewer positive results.

The Indians were initially approached to recreate the stunt. Team president Gabe Paul turned it down flat. At the time, Cleveland was also home to a professional slow-pitch softball team. (Really.) The Competitors were owned by advertising impresario Ted Stepien, who had also become majority owner earlier that year of the Cavaliers. The Competitors would be happy to participate, and Stepien himself, never shy about publicity, would stand at the top of the Terminal Tower and throw the softballs down to members of the team to catch.

And so during lunchtime on June 24, 1980, Stepien leaned out from the 52nd floor of the tower, looking down at a crowd around 5,000 that had gathered at ground level to watch. "This is bad," he said (as later recounted in *Cleveland Magazine*). "I'm really going to hurt somebody." His first throw hit a parked car. The second throw hit retiree Russell Murphy in the shoulder. He declined medical attention. The third hit Gayle Falinski, a downtown worker who'd been watching from the sidewalk across the street. She was shielding her eyes from the noonday sun, and the ball struck her wrist, breaking it. (All in all, it could have been far worse; it was estimated the softballs were traveling 144 mph on their way down.) The next ball bounced on the sidewalk "about 40 feet in the air," recalled Dan Coughlin, who covered the event for the *Plain Dealer*. Finally, Mike Zarefoss, a corrections officer who played for Stepien's softball team, caught one.

Stepien sent Falinski flowers and invited her to lunch—and two years later settled her lawsuit for $35,875.

TYRONE HILL RENTS A LIMO

Following the Cavs' 97-72 loss in the regular-season finale in Charlotte on April 23, 1995, the team hopped on their charter flight for a return to Cleveland.

It was a plane ride they'd never forget—and not in a good way.

Players said the flight dropped a thousand feet in a matter of seconds, and three minutes of turbulence passed like an eternity. Some players said their lives flashed before their eyes. But nobody was shaken like Tyrone Hill. "When I got off that plane, I called up everybody I knew that I had been bad to and said I was sorry," he later told the *Plain Dealer*. "I tell you, I lost every bit of my manhood that day."

The Cavs were due to open the playoffs at Madison Square Garden against the Knicks on April 27. Hill swore he'd never fly again, and rented a limousine to drive him the 475 miles from Cleveland to Manhattan. It was a nine-hour drive, no doubt leaving him sapped.

In the opener, Hill was thoroughly outplayed by Charles Oakley, with just seven points and eight rebounds in a 103-79 loss.

Things didn't go much better for him for the rest of the series, as the Cavs lost to the Knicks, three games to one. Hill, the Cavs' lone all-star that season, averaged 8.5 points and 5.7 rebounds per game in the series, far below his regular-season averages.

Perhaps he had limo-lag.

"THE DECISION"

On July 8, 2010, millions of viewers turned on ESPN for the resolution of a cliffhanger that, while not quite as big as "Who shot J.R.?", might have been on a par with "Who shot Mr. Burns?" It was LeBron James taking the unprecedented step of an hour-long television special to announce "The Decision."

James, an Akron native, had been drafted first overall by the Cavs in 2003 and in his seven-year career in Cleveland had already cemented himself as the best player to wear a Cavs uniform. He had guided the team to five straight playoff appearances, including their first NBA Finals appearance, and two 60-win seasons. He was also heralded for demonstrating wisdom beyond his years, keeping his head on straight, staying out of trouble and being an engaged citizen in addition to his on-court prowess.

In 2007, he had signed a three-year extension, meaning he would become a free agent in 2010.

Then, following an ignominious end to the 2010 postseason, with a loss to the Celtics in the Eastern Conference Semifinals, the real games began in Cleveland.

Over the course of several weeks, LeBron entertained offers from interested parties in the IMG building in downtown Cleveland. In addition to the Cavs, he heard from the Bulls, Knicks, Nets, Heat and Clippers. Finally, he was ready to make his Decision, which by this time had taken on the weight of a papal bull.

Sitting in the Boys & Girls Club of Greenwich, Conn., the location chosen for the hourlong ESPN special, LeBron made small talk with Jim Gray—who'd planted the seed for the special during that year's playoffs—before getting to the most important question, announcing he'd be "taking [his] talents to South Beach" to play for the Heat. In Miami, a superteam was being assembled. LeBron would team up with Dwyane Wade and Chris Bosh, who was coming to the Heat from Toronto. (Probably not coincidentally, they were all part of the 2003 NBA Draft class and teammates on the U.S. Olympic team in 2008.) They were being celebrated as the NBA's next dynasty. But the reaction to the special itself was swift, and from many corners, brutal.

"An orgy of excess," the *Washington Post* called it. Rick Telander of the *Chicago Sun-Times* spoke of LeBron's "pomp, phoniness, pseudo-humility and rehearsed innocence." The *Boston Globe* excoriated the move on its editorial page. Years later, it came out that NBA Commissioner David Stern, seeing what was about to happen, tried to stop the special. About the only beneficiary of The Decision was the Boys & Girls Club, which got $2.5 million in donations for hosting the special.

But a funny thing happened during LeBron's time in Miami. The decision to go to Miami was sound. But The Decision? He realized he had stepped in it. He talked at length about it with Lee Jenkins, who profiled him when he was named *Sports Illustrated* sportsperson of the year in 2012, after finally breaking through and winning his first title. And LeBron called Jenkins again, in the summer of 2014, for the story in *Sports Illustrated* where he announced that he was returning to Cleveland—a far more low-key approach.

The Decision has had implications to this day, changing the balance of power within the league, not among teams, but between teams and the players themselves. The Decision set the stage for seemingly no end of free agent moves. And one of those, of course, was LeBron's return to Cleveland in 2014 and the resulting end to the city's 52-year title drought. So maybe it wasn't all bad.

"THE ORANGE IS ORANGER"

In 2012, Jimmy Haslam bought the Browns. One of his first actions was to hire Alec Scheiner away from the Dallas Cowboys to be team president. The last person to hold that title for the Browns had been Mike Holmgren, who was given sway over football operations. Under Haslam's ownership, those duties initially fell to team CEO Joe Banner and Personnel Director (later General Manager)

Mike Lombardi. Scheiner's job was to improve the "fan experience"—the catchall term for everything that happens when you go to a football game except the game itself.

The moves in Haslam's ownership make sense if you look at the Browns as an undervalued asset. Ticket prices were increased, not reflective of any increase in payroll or other expenses, but simply to bring them in line with other other NFL teams' prices. New scoreboards were installed at the stadium (the shape of the scoreboard, some noted, seemed similar to Haslam's home state of Tennessee). A drumline was introduced, and mascots appeared: Chomps the dog, and the return of the Brownie the elf. And plans were made almost immediately to update the team logo and uniforms.

The Browns had been formed in the All-American Conference in 1946, and their uniforms had remained relatively unchanged since: brown or white jerseys and white pants. When the team transitioned from leather helmets to plastic ones, the helmets were orange. There were some dalliances with orange pants and special orange shirts, and eventually, brown pants were incorporated, but nothing really took hold. Haslam and Scheiner decided the team's look needed freshened up.

It started in February 2015, when a new logo was revealed. At least, they said it was a new logo. It didn't look much different. "The traditional non-decaled helmet now presents a stronger, more energetic orange and a brown facemask that provides a tougher edge, three prime characteristics that depict the team and its fans," the team explained in a news release. "It is complemented by a contemporary, powerful wordmark that also incorporates a stronger, bolder font."

Also, the Browns' alternate Dawg Pound logo was reimagined . . . much like Poochie was added to *Itchy and Scratchy* on *The Simpsons*. And the orange was given a brighter, richer hue to match "the passion of our fans and city." In other words, as fans noted, the orange was oranger.

"Completely underwhelming," said the *Washington Post*. "Just as boring as before," said *USA Today*. The sports website Grantland mocked the change with a purported exclusive for "The Re-Oranging of the Cleveland Browns."

The new logo was just a prelude. Two months later, new uniforms were unveiled at the convention center in downtown Cleveland to great fanfare.

"I don't think they're an extreme difference but they're different enough," Scheiner said at the time, in a statement distributed to the media by the Browns. "You won't mistake them for our old uniforms."

He wasn't wrong. The initial reaction was actually sort of positive. And with the Browns coming off their best season in seven years, maybe fans would be receptive to a little change. But then the team went 4-44 over the next three seasons, souring any good feelings there might have been for the new togs. The team kept the uniforms for as long as they had to (NFL rules required teams to keep uniforms for at least five years), then in 2019 announced that they would change uniforms again the following year. By then, Scheiner was gone. He resigned after the 2015 season, which had included an attempt to expand his power base by reaching into football operations. (News accounts said he went so far as to watch game film with then-coach Mike Pettine.)

In 2020, during the Covid-19 pandemic, the Browns unveiled *new* new uniforms in a socially distant way, online.

"I think we got it right this time," co-owner Dee Haslam told Cleveland.com's Mary Kay Cabot.

The new new uniforms looked an awful lot like the ones from before the 2015 change.

GPODAWUND

The Browns were 0-7 heading into a home matchup against the New York Jets on Oct. 30, 2016, but the 67,341 fans in attendance were hyped. The stadium was packed. The crowd was electric, and for an added boost, the team would unfurl a giant banner in the east end zone reading, "This is the DAWG POUND." Immediately after, the crowd would give a mighty roar and the invigorated team would come out and get their first win of the season.

Theoretically.

The giant banner was actually three separate banners that would combine to spell out "This is the" (in small letters) and "DAWG POUND" (in huge letters). But apparently, two banners got confused. So instead of Dawg Pound, we were introduced to a new word: GPODAWUND.

The Browns were so inept, they couldn't even get a banner right.

Denizens of Northeast Ohio, used to all varieties of incompetence from their football team, took it in stride. GPODAWUND T-shirts were printed up, and a local microbrewery introduced a GPODAWUND Brown Ale.

USA Today said the banner screw-up perfectly encapsulated the Browns' season. NBC Sports called it "The most Browns move ever." NFL.com noted that everything may be coming up roses for Cleveland as of late, but the banners reminded everyone that "The Browns are still the Browns."

Wait—everything coming up roses? What made things so good for Cleveland? Well, earlier that summer, the Cavs rallied from a 3-1 deficit in the NFL Finals to beat the 73-win Golden State Warriors to bring Cleveland its first major league sports title in 52 years. And that night, the Indians would be playing the Cubs in Game 5 of the World Series, holding a 3-1 series lead. Even if they lost that night, they would still have two more chances—both at home—to close out the Cubs and win the team's first title in nearly 70 years.

Well, we all know how that turned out. I'm not saying the Indians wilted under the curse of GPODAWUND.

But I'm not saying they didn't, either.

ATHLETES BEHAVING BADLY

"I am not a role model," Charles Barkley famously said in a 1993 Nike TV commercial.

Some athletes are. Bob Feller became the first major leaguer to join the armed forces the day after the Japanese attack on Pearl Harbor. Akron's I Promise School is a monumental philanthropic undertaking by LeBron James and his eponymous foundation. As a student at the University of Texas, future Browns quarterback Colt McCoy helped save a neighbor's life while he was having a seizure.

But despite their feats on the field, athletes are human beings, which means like anyone else, they can be capable of bad behavior. Sometimes REALLY odd bad behavior.

JOHNNY ALLEN'S SWEATSHIRT INCIDENT

As a pitcher for the Yankees, Johnny Allen had a blazing fastball and a curve that looked like it fell off a table. But he also had a temperament that could, diplomatically, be called mercurial. "He expects to win every time he pitches, and if he doesn't win, he may turn on anybody," Yankees trainer Doc Painter told the *St. Petersburg Times* in 1964, five years after Allen's death.

In four years in the Bronx, Allen went 50-19, but he wore out his welcome, arguing regularly with manager Joe McCarthy. After the 1935 season, Allen was dealt to the Indians. He won 20 games for the Indians in 1936 (although all the headlines went to the teenage phenom scout Cy Slapnicka had unearthed in Iowa—Bob Feller), but lost 10, his most losses in a season to that point. He also had to be restrained by umpires from going after Tigers manager Del Baker after that team had heckled him in an outing, and was fined $250 and threatened with suspension for tearing up a hotel hallway in Boston.

The following year, Allen had won 15 straight games and was going for the American League record for consecutive wins (also against the Tigers) when Hank Greenberg hit a grounder right through the legs of Indians third baseman Odell Hale, driving in what turned out to be the only run of the game. Once again, Allen had to be restrained. Actually, twice again: Indians manager Steve O'Neill came between Allen and Hale first in the locker room, and then again later in the dining car on the train ride back to Cleveland.

Following the season, O'Neill was fired as manager and replaced by Oscar Vitt, who had managed the Yankees' top minor league affiliate in Newark. Vitt picked up right where O'Neill left off, holding Allen back after he was ejected from an April game by umpire Bill McGowan.

"Whenever McGowan works a game I pitch," Allen told the *Plain Dealer*, "there's always been a lot of petty, sniveling work going on. I've got a belly full of it."

McGowan was also behind the plate on June 7, 1938, when Allen was pitching for the Indians against the Red Sox at Fenway Park. With one on and two out in the bottom of the first, Jimmie Foxx launched a game-tying home run, but Allen retired shortstop/manager Joe Cronin to end the inning. Cronin complained to McGowan about the sweatshirt Allen was wearing under his jersey. There were slits cut in it, and the sleeves were loose, causing batters to lose sight of the ball on its way to the plate. (The American League rulebook specifically forbade pitchers from wearing shirts "with ragged or slit sleeves which have the effect of confusing the batter.")

Allen was sent to change his shirt. Game action stopped for five minutes. Then ten minutes. Finally, Vitt and shortstop Lyn Lary went into the locker room and found an indignant Allen, who had no intention of changing his shirt. *Plain Dealer* writer Gordon Cobbledick, in a front-page story, called it "one of the most astounding exhibitions of insubordination in the history of baseball."

Vitt adjusted on the fly, bringing in Bill Zuber in relief. Zuber didn't fare well, but after him Johnny Humphries did, and the Indians held on for a 7-5 win. Irate, Vitt fined Allen $250.

"I wore that shirt all last season without anyone complaining," Allen said, according to the biography *Fiery Fast-Baller* by Wint Capel.

Ultimately, Higbee's, the downtown department store, offered $500 for the sweatshirt and put it on display in its window. (It was probably just a coincidence that the store's director, Chuck Bradley, was a minority owner of the Indians. His brother, Alva, was the majority owner.) The shirt was eventually displayed at the Baseball Hall of Fame.

"A department store in Cleveland just long-distanced me with an offer of almost five hundred bucks for that shirt McGowan objected to up at Boston," said Allen. "And I sold it to 'em so as to prove Mrs. Allen never raised any foolish children. I got fined two fifty but I'm getting a net profit."

Despite the incident, Allen remained on a tear, starting the season 13-1. Then, an arm injury curtailed his effectiveness down the stretch, and he finished the season 14-8. He would never win more than 10 games in a season again.

DENNIS ECKERSLEY GETS
DUMPED AND TRADED

They were supposed to be stars. They were supposed to be friends.

Rick Manning and Dennis Eckersley met as teammates on the Indians' Class A team in Reno in 1972. Both had been drafted that year—Manning with the Indians' first pick and Eckersley in the third round. Manning was initially thought of as a shortstop—a notion he quickly dispelled with his infield play—but Eckersley was already showing his talent as a pitcher.

Eckersley made the big leagues first, in 1975. With his sidearm fastball, wicked curve, long, flowing hair and intense demeanor, he could actually frighten opposing hitters. Later that season, Manning was brought up from Triple-A, now as a center fielder.

Once again, Eckersley and Manning were inseparable. Both benefitted from the tutelage of manager Frank Robinson. Eckersley threw a no-hitter on Memorial Day 1977. Less than a week later, Manning hurt his back sliding into second. Eckersley would be named to the All-Star team, but Manning, despite a lackluster year, would end up rich. The Indians sent Manning a contract that included a 25-percent pay cut, a violation of the MLB collective bargaining agreement. As a result, Manning entered into MLB's nascent free agency. The Indians ended up signing him to a five-year, $2.5 million deal to keep him in Cleveland.

During spring training 1978, it became known that Eckersley was being shopped around, and on March 31, he was dealt to the Boston Red Sox. The Indians got four players in return, the centerpiece being Ted Cox, who is still the record holder for consecutive hits to start a major league career (6). Also coming to Cleveland were Bo Diaz, Rick Wise and Mike Paxton.

But why would a team want to trade a young pitcher coming off an All-Star season?

Ostensibly, the deal was done because scouts and coaches

were concerned that Eckersley's sidewinding delivery would actually shorten his career. But gradually, word got out about the real reason. The day Eckersley found out he was dealt to Boston, his wife, Denise—they had been high school sweethearts, he the jock and she the cheerleading captain—filed for divorce.

Eckersley got no decision in each of his first four starts, but he recovered to win 20 games for the Red Sox—who needed every one of those wins just to get into a one-game playoff against the Yankees, which they lost. Local newspapers referred obliquely to Eckersley's divorce, which was playing out in Cuyahoga County court. And eventually, word got around why the divorce happened.

Denise had met another man—as it turns out, years earlier. It was Rick Manning.

Manning, recovering from his back injury, was staying with the Eckersleys at their home. Meanwhile, Eckersley was in the throes of a drinking problem. "We had to trade someone before the whole thing blew up in our faces," Indians executive Gabe Paul told Terry Pluto in an interview for the book *The Curse of Rocky Colavito*. Paul said that Manning's trade value was down due to the injury, and he really thought Manning would bounce back and be a star. "We traded the wrong guy."

Manning went on to have a lengthy career. The Indians dealt him in 1983 to Milwaukee, and he retired following the 1987 season. Ultimately, he and Denise got married—and divorced. Eckersley, meanwhile, had his own demons to slay. He did develop arm troubles, and the Red Sox traded him to the Cubs, where he looked better—helping them to a division title and appearing in an NLCS game in 1984—but sunk deeper into alcoholism. After a stint in rehab in January 1987, he ended up in Oakland—his hometown—pitching for the Athletics. Their rotation was full, so he transitioned into the bullpen, finding his second act as a Hall of Fame closer.

All four of the players the Indians got combined didn't have the career Eckersley went on to have.

Manning has been part of the Indians broadcast crew since 1990. Understandably, he is reluctant to talk about his first marriage.

Eckersley returned to Boston at the end of his career, and then joined the Red Sox broadcast team. On-air during a game in 2018 he was asked if he had been friendly with any players despite being in a rivalry. "I don't know about a rivalry," he said. "I had a friend who stole my wife—how about that?"

HALL FIGHTS HOYNSIE IN THE CLUBHOUSE

When the Indians dealt star pitcher Rick Sutcliffe to the Cubs in 1984, the centerpiece of the deal for them was slugging outfielder Joe Carter. But another important acquisition was Mel Hall, who'd finished third the year before in National League Rookie of the Year voting.

The deal paid dividends for the Indians for years to come. Not only did Joe Carter provide some pop for the Indians' lineup, but the haul the team got when they traded him to the Padres five years later set up future success for another decade. By the time the Indians traded Carter after the 1989 season, Hall was also gone—to the great relief of just about everyone in Cleveland.

Longtime *Plain Dealer* baseball writer Paul Hoynes wrote in a 2009 story that Hall "oozed a casual recklessness," and it eventually caught up to him: That year, Hall was convicted of multiple sex crimes and sentenced to 45 years in prison.

Hall had nicknamed himself the Gunfighter, for his role as the Indians' enforcer. He made no bones about wanting to leave Cleveland after the 1988 season, and his departure was hastened by him bringing both his wife and girlfriend to spring training in 1989. They found each other by the pool at the hotel and fought in front of Indians president Hank Peters' wife and granddaughter. (Hall was traded to the Yankees shortly thereafter.)

In 1987, Hall had been sued for child support. He had also sued for damages following a car wreck that injured him in spring training in 1985, limiting him to just 23 games that year. Hoynes had written about both lawsuits, and was going about his business one Sunday morning at Cleveland Stadium when manager Pat Corrales told him, "You better get out of here, there's a bounty on your head."

Hoynes, taking the advice, turned to leave . . . and suddenly found himself face-to-face with Hall, who proceeded to tell him, loudly and profanely, exactly what he thought of him. Hoynes offered a rebuttal, and before long, the two were on the ground in front of Carmen Castillo's locker. Otis Nixon had to pull Hall off Hoynes, who bore no grudges.

"Mel Hall was an interesting guy," he recalled years later for Baseball Prospectus. "He almost killed me once in the locker room."

Strangely enough, Hoynes said he had a great working relationship with Hall after that incident.

SIR CHARLES FIGHTS IN THE FLATS

Wherever Charles Barkley went, controversy followed.

He had a rivalry with Bill Laimbeer (more on him later) that seemed more suited for the boxing ring than the basketball court. (The two famously sent up their frequent brawls with cameo appearances in the 1991 movie *Hot Shots*.) He once spit on a girl in the stands. (He was aiming for a heckler whom he said was using racial slurs.) He said he was misquoted in his own autobiography!

But if nothing else, he was self-aware. "I heard Tonya Harding called herself the Charles Barkley of figure skating," he said in 1994, according to *Sports Illustrated*. "I was going to sue for defamation of character, but then I realized I had no character!"

Barkley was one of the best basketball players of the 1980s, so it was a slam-dunk that he'd be on the 1992 Olympic basketball team, the first to include NBA players. The "Dream Team," essentially an all-star team coached by Chuck Daly (more on him later, too), blew through the competition for a gold medal. Barkley was one of five players from that team who were on the 1996 Olympic team as well.

On July 7, 1996, the Olympic team was in Cleveland for a tune-up against Brazil. They were coming off a six-point win the day before against a collegiate team—closer than they would have liked—and blew the doors off Brazil, 109-68.

According to police reports, Barkley had that fighting instinct early that morning as well. He was at the Basement, a nightclub in the Flats, with the Pacers' Reggie Miller, another member of the Olympic team. Words were exchanged between Barkley and a pair of men from upstate New York, and one of them, Jeb Tyler, said Barkley beat him up.

Both Tyler and Barkley filed police reports, but ultimately, no criminal charges were filed. "I really don't want to see Charles Barkley get arrested and detained for this," Tyler said in the *Plain Dealer.* "He would have to come back to Cleveland and get arraigned in two weeks. He'd miss the Olympics."

But Tyler did file a civil suit, seeking a total of more than $50,000 in compensatory and punitive damages. Barkley returned in July 1997 for a trial. Tyler offered to settle the case for $12,000, but Barkley had no urge to do so, as he told the Associated Press after the verdict: "Why should I give him $12,000? He didn't earn it. He doesn't get rebounds. He doesn't get hit in the head by Karl Malone."

Ultimately, Barkley was exonerated at trial. He'd spent more than the $12,000 that would have settled it on lawyers, but he said he went to trial on principle. Barkley emerged victorious from the courthouse in Cleveland, and met his adoring public, shaking hands and signing autographs for fans.

Chastened, he vowed never to fight again.

Just kidding! He threw a guy out a window in Orlando that October.

ALBERT BELLE

The Indians' history has been full of intimidating hitters. Napoleon Lajoie—so good they named the team after him—was one of the first modern major leaguers to get 3,000 hits. Tris Speaker was as good at the plate as he was patrolling the large expanse of grass in League Park. Al Rosen came within an eyelash of a Triple Crown.

And in the 1990s, there was no hitter more feared than Albert Belle—as much for his personality as his offensive prowess.

Belle, a native of Shreveport, La., played college baseball at Louisiana State University. He was regarded as a top prospect—or would be, were it not for his temper. In the Southeastern Conference tournament, Belle, then known as Joey, a diminutive of his middle name, Jojuan, ran off the field to chase down a heckler who was yelling racial slurs. Two teammates had to keep him from going into the stands, and he was suspended.

Atlanta Braves manager Bobby Cox told his personnel director he'd fire him if he drafted Belle. The Indians were desperate enough to take a chance on him, but they didn't have a first-round pick, and he had first-round talent. "Nobody's going to take him in the first round," Indians General Manager Joe Klein said, according to the book *Endless Summers* by Jack Torry. He turned out to be right, and the Indians snagged Belle in the second round of the 1987 MLB Draft.

Belle tore up minor league pitching—and clubhouses; his intensity and perfectionism often boiled over into rage—and made his major league debut in 1989. The following year, he spent 10 weeks in alcohol rehab at the Cleveland Clinic and was limited to nine games with the Indians.

By 1991, he had a renewed focus on his game—and he was now going by Albert, not Joey, reflecting the change he'd undergone. But the anger remained. Media accounts at the time reported that a fan said, "Hey, Joey, keg party at my house!" Belle threw a ball at him, hitting him in the chest. In 1993, he got into a fight with a Baltimore-area man at Jillian's in the Flats. In 1995, when he didn't supply some kids with candy on Halloween, his Euclid home was egged. He then tried to chase them down with his Ford Explorer. (He was ultimately convicted of reckless operation of a motor vehicle and fined.)

He was no more pleasant with the media. He blew off an interview with Roy Firestone. He berated Hannah Storm in the locker room prior to a game in what turned out to be the only World Series he would play in, in 1995 (for his actions, he was fined $50,000 and ordered to undergo counseling). He threw a baseball at photographer Tony Tomsic, a former *Cleveland Press* hand who took photos for *Sports Illustrated*. He told a reporter from the same magazine, "*Sports Illustrated* can kiss my black ass." He almost picked a fight in the clubhouse with *Plain Dealer* writer Bud Shaw. In 1995, the *Baltimore Sun* called Belle "infamous for his treatment of writers and broadcasters" and related his statement to a Chicago radio reporter: "I don't know you, I don't want to know you, I don't want to talk to you."

That truculence likely cost him the 1995 American League MVP award. He finished second that year to Mo Vaughn of the Boston Red Sox. "If you believe that personality was a major factor in the AL MVP voting announced last week, you are absolutely correct," wrote Buster Olney in the *Baltimore Sun*. "If you believe that part of the reason Boston Red Sox first baseman Mo Vaughn won the voting is that he's a good guy, you are absolutely correct. If you believe that a major reason Cleveland Indians left fielder Albert Belle lost is that he's a jerk, you are absolutely correct."

Belle was equally combative with players—and it didn't matter if they were on his team or not. Teammate Kenny Lofton nicknamed Belle "Mr. Freeze" because he liked the air conditioning turned down to ice cold. Lofton said other players turned it back up, but Belle kept turning it down—finally taking a baseball bat to the thermostat. Belle also took a bat to Lofton's boom box once.

In the 1992 and 1993 seasons, he served three-game suspensions for charging the mound. In 1996, he famously trucked Fernando

Vina while running toward second base in an effort to break up a double play. For that, he was only suspended two games—but fined $25,000. Longtime Indians executive Bob DiBiasio later recalled that disciplinary matters were handled in the league office in New York, and it seemed like every time they came to town, they had to report to the league office because of Albert Belle.

But his offensive prowess was unquestionable. In a lineup littered with great hitters, Belle was a breed apart. In 1991, he hit 28 home runs, and never hit fewer than 30 in any other season he played for the Indians. Three times he led the American League in runs batted in, and for one of those times, he led the entire major league. His career year was 1995, when, in a season shortened to 144 games, he hit 50 home runs and 52 doubles. He remains the only player to have that kind of 50-50 season.

To borrow the quote attributed to Franklin Roosevelt, Albert Belle might have been a son of a bitch, but he was our son of a bitch. At least, until 1996, when he took advantage of his free agency and signed a five-year, $55 million contract with the Tribe's American League Central rivals, the White Sox. Belle's departure from Cleveland was upsetting for the loss of his bat in the lineup, but on some level, a lot of fans breathed a sigh of relief that they didn't have to defend his behavior any longer.

Belle spent three years on the South Side of Chicago. His contract stipulated that he was to be one of the three highest-paid players in the league, and because the White Sox couldn't—or wouldn't—meet that, he became a free agent, and signed with Baltimore. His productivity dropped precipitously due to a degenerative hip condition that ultimately forced his retirement following the 2000 season.

He re-established cordial relationships with DiBiasio and other members of the Tribe's front office, visiting spring training in 2012 and getting a bobblehead in his honor the following year. In 2016, he was inducted into the team's hall of fame. (Cooperstown has not come calling for Belle; any chance of a plaque at the Baseball Hall of Fame rests with the veterans committee. His candidacy is probably borderline, but the writers who vote for inductees—who he'd spurned in his career—were unlikely to give him the benefit of the doubt. He dropped off the writers' ballot after two years.)

He opted not to return to Cleveland for the induction.

Some things never change.

THE DRAFT PICK WHO GOT ARRESTED

The 2001 NFL Draft was not a good one for the Browns. I mean, most haven't been, but this one was especially bad. With the third overall pick, the Browns reached for defensive lineman Gerard Warren. (Published reports later said that the staff had preferred Richard Seymour, who was drafted sixth by the Patriots. He went on to become a seven-time Pro Bowler, a key part of three Super Bowl winners in New England and a Hall of Famer. The only way Warren will get to a Pro Bowl is by buying a ticket. Oh, and the Browns passed on future Hall of Famer LaDainian Tomlinson, who went one spot before Seymour, too.)

Quincy Morgan, a wide receiver taken by the Browns in the second round, and Anthony Henry, a defensive back taken in the fourth round, both put together decent NFL careers. But one player, Jeremiah Pharms, didn't even play a down in the NFL.

Pharms, a linebacker from the University of Washington, was taken in the fifth round. Coach Butch Davis said at the time Pharms was "intriguing," and had received nothing but glowing reports about him from coach Rick Neuheisel. He'd married his high school sweetheart while at college, and they had three children together. "While his Washington teammates were out socializing on Friday and Saturday nights, Jeremiah Pharms was home changing diapers," Susan Vinella wrote in a *Plain Dealer* story introducing Browns fans to Pharms after the draft.

But with his bags packed, ready for his rookie minicamp, Pharms was arrested and charged with robbery by police in Washington. The Browns (whose security director at the time was the retired Secret Service director) had no idea. Davis said because it was a fifth-round pick, he wasn't put through the paces of a full background check, and he relied on interviews with Pharms' coaches at Washington. "Apparently, the sleuthing stops after the second or third round," Bill Livingston wrote in the *Plain Dealer*.

Neuheisel and athletic director Barbara Hedges both claimed not to know Pharms was being investigated for his role in a robbery that occurred more than a year before his name was called at the NFL Draft.

"I've been accused of knowing and not divulging, and I can categorically say that's false," Neuheisel said at the time, according to the *Seattle Times*. "I can only apologize and say that I was in the same company as everyone else who did not know."

Pharms was charged with first-degree robbery for allegedly buying pot from a dealer on campus, and then returning later, pistol-whipping and shooting the dealer and taking more than $1,000 worth of marijuana. He entered an Alford plea—which is not a guilty plea but admits there is enough evidence to lead to a guilty verdict—and ended up serving more than two years in prison for the crime. He referred to his stint as "extended training camp" in interviews with Seattle newspapers, and participated in Washington's pro day in 2005.

Among the NFL representatives there was Terry Robiskie, then the Browns' wide receivers coach. Pharms was spreading around brochures about his return.

Robiskie declined.

THREE BROWNS PLAYERS, TWO CITIES AND A BUNCH OF ARRESTS

Jeremiah Pharms wasn't the only Browns player to get in trouble in 2001. In fact, he wasn't even the only Browns rookie that year to run afoul of the law.

The week of Thanksgiving in 2001, three Browns players were arrested within a matter of hours—in two separate states!

Cleveland police spotted a pickup truck speeding and weaving in and out of traffic on West 25th Street on the evening of Nov. 19. It was the day after the Browns had beaten the Ravens to move to 5-4, with the playoffs still in reach in Butch Davis' first season as coach. Police stopped the truck near Walton Avenue in Ohio City. The Browns' Mike Sellers was driving and Lamar Chapman, a defensive back on injured reserve, was in the passenger seat. Police said they found bags of marijuana as well as three spent cigars in the car. A dollar bill was also believed to contain trace amounts of cocaine.

Early Tuesday morning, a party was breaking up in Pittsburgh's Strip District, a neighborhood that by day is known for its fresh food markets, but at night is more notorious for its nightclubs. Steelers wide receiver Plaxico Burress was hosting a party Monday night at Donzi's, a club on a barge. Among those in attendance was Browns defensive lineman Gerard Warren and starting tight end O.J. Santiago. As the party was breaking up, police noticed a man, later identified as Percy Blue, smoking what appeared to be a blunt in a Chevrolet Suburban with the rear driver's side door open.

The vehicle belonged to Warren. A search yielded suspected drugs and a Glock .45-caliber pistol. Warren was charged immediately with possession of an unlicensed firearm. (Please savor the irony of Gerard Warren being arrested for an unlicensed firearm at a party thrown by Plaxico Burress. At least Warren didn't shoot himself with it, like Plex did in 2008.)

Teammates were low-key but supportive.

"It's how you bounce back from it," safety Devin Bush said afterward in a press conference with local media. "This is an opportunity for us to rally."

Warren, Sellers and Chapman were suspended for the following game—which the Browns won against the Bengals—and when Sellers was expecting to be reinstated the following week, he was instead released, a move that stunned his agent and teammates. Following the Bengals win, the Browns lost their next four to fall out of playoff contention.

Although Sellers and Chapman both initially faced felony charges, Sellers ended up pleading guilty to driving under the

influence, and Chapman pleaded to possession of drug parapher-
nalia. Chapman was released by the Browns the following summer,
and never played a down in the NFL again, but Sellers, after two
seasons in the CFL, returned to the Redskins, the team that drafted
him, and made the 2009 Pro Bowl as a fullback.

Santiago was charged with drug possession in December for
the incident at the party, and those charges were knocked down to
disorderly conduct, for which he paid a fine. Warren's gun charge
was also reduced to a misdemeanor, and he was sentenced to one
year's probation. Warren's on-field production declined in 2003,
and he refocused on football enough that while he never lived up
to the hype of his early nickname, Big Money, he was able to put
together an 11-year career, even if he was dealt away from Cleveland, for which he still held fondness.

"I was misunderstood in Cleveland," Warren said at Super Bowl
media day in 2012, when he was a member of the Patriots. "All I
ever wanted to do was win."

WILLIAM GREEN FALLS ON A KNIFE

In 2002, everything seemed to fall into place for the Browns. In
their fourth year of rebirth, they'd not only finished with a winning
record, but made the playoffs for the first time since their return in
1999.

At least some of that success was due to rookie running back
William Green. The Browns drafted him 16th overall. Like he did
with Gerard Warren the year before, Butch Davis went all-in on
Green. Team President Carmen Policy was not as sold, noting
Green's history, which included a troubled childhood (both his
parents had died of AIDS while he was a teenager) and two suspensions during his college career at Boston College. But in Davis'
eyes, the talent (he was touted as the best running back in that
year's draft) was worth the risk.

Green put together an exemplary rookie year, eventually becoming the featured back, running for 887 yards and six touchdowns, the last a 64-yard run in the regular season finale. The Browns were clinging to a one-point lead with less than four minutes to play when Green found a lane and broke loose for the score against the Falcons, leading to one of Browns radio voice Jim Donovan's most beloved calls, yelling "RUN, WILLIAM, RUN!" as Green tore down the sidelines.

Green could only hold his troubles at bay for so long, unfortunately. The following year, the fire wasn't there. His problems with substance abuse led to a traffic stop in Westlake, where he was charged with marijuana possession and driving under the influence. He was suspended by the Browns and the NFL.

Westlake police were called to his home on November 19, 2003, by his fiancée Asia Gray, a former Miss Pleasantville in their home state of New Jersey. Green had sustained a puncture wound. He said he was carrying some household items up the steps and tripped, accidentally stabbing himself with a knife he was carrying.

It was hard to believe because as a running back, Green was normally sure-footed. It was even harder to believe because he'd been stabbed in the back.

Ultimately, Gray was charged with domestic violence and was given probation. Green served three days in jail for the DUI but remained suspended by the league through the end of the season. Davis resigned as the 2004 season drew to a close, and Green lost his biggest supporter in Cleveland. Terry Robiskie finished out the season as interim head coach before the Browns hired former Patriots assistant Romeo Crennel, who didn't think he could trust Green—but kept him on the roster, at least initially.

Green's NFL career ended after just four seasons. He ended up going through rehab, and is now a minister and motivational speaker. He lives in his native New Jersey with his eight children and his wife—the former Asia Gray.

WHO IS FAUSTO CARMONA?

The 2007 baseball season ended on a sour note in Cleveland, as the Indians coughed up a 3-1 lead in the American League Championship Series against the Red Sox. (They were hardly alone in that respect. The Red Sox had come back from 3-1 in the 1986 American League Championship Series against the Angels, and were down a seemingly insurmountable three games to none in the 2004 ALCS against the Yankees.) But there were still bright spots—among them Fausto Carmona.

Carmona was signed weeks after his 17th birthday by the Indians from his native Dominican Republic in 2000. He made his way through the team's minor league system and debuted with the Tribe in 2006. He beat the Tigers in his first start, giving up just one earned run in six innings' work. It turned out to be his only win that season.

After the Indians traded Bob Wickman to the Braves, they attempted to use Carmona as the closer. It did not go well. He had three blown saves (including two on back-to-back nights at Fenway Park) and four losses in a seven-game span, which included game-winning home runs to David Ortiz and Ivan Rodriguez. He was optioned to Buffalo, and then recalled when the rosters expanded in September. He finished the season with a 1-10 record and a 5.42 ERA.

The following year, manager Eric Wedge planned to use him as a spot starter, but an injury to Cliff Lee in spring training pushed Carmona into the rotation. (Lee went 5-8 in an injury-plagued year, with a 6.29 ERA. It's downright aggravating to wonder if the Indians could have advanced past the Red Sox had he performed at a level of previous seasons—let alone the Cy Young season he'd have in 2008.)

Carmona responded admirably. The ace of the staff was CC Sabathia, but Carmona was right there with him. In a season where he ended up winning the Cy Young Award, Sabathia went

19-7. Carmona went 19-8, and finished fourth in Cy Young voting (admittedly, with just seven votes; it was a two-horse race between Sabathia and Boston's Josh Beckett, who led the American League with 20 wins). And unlike Sabathia, whom everyone seemed to know would test the free agent market following the 2008 season, Carmona was under team control, signing a four-year, $15 million extension—with three club option years—early in 2008. At the time, Indians assistant general manager Chris Antonetti noted it was the largest guaranteed contract given to a major leaguer with one year of service time. All told, the contract could have been worth $48 million for a pitcher whom everyone thought, at age 24, hadn't even entered his prime.

But he never reached the heights of 2007 again. In fact, he never had a winning record as a pitcher again, and won more than eight games in a season only once more (in 2009, when he went 13-14 and made his only All-Star Team). Still, the Indians picked up his 2012 club option.

That January, he reapplied for a work visa in his native Dominican Republic. After leaving the U.S. Embassy in the nation's capital of Santo Domingo, he was arrested by Dominican police on a charge of identity fraud. He made bail quickly, but his passport was forfeited. He was unable to leave his native country for spring training.

Details soon emerged on who Fausto Carmona actually was. His name was Roberto Hernandez-Heredia, and he was 31, not 28 as stated on his birth certificate, which turned out to be a forgery. The pitcher everyone thought was just coming into his prime when he signed a hefty contract turned out to be at the peak of his career with that miraculous 2007 season. There was nowhere to go but down.

In the Dominican Republic, baseball was seen as a way out of poverty, and there was a vibrant industry of hangers-on, unofficial scouts and managers called *buscones*, who would shave a few years off a prospect's age to make him more enticing. Hernandez-Heredia was one of those players. (The real Fausto Carmona had himself gone on to another identity.) Major League Baseball had tightened identity verification—as had the nation at large since 9/11—but Carmona, er, Hernandez-Heredia had been signed before those safeguards were in place.

It took several months, but Hernandez-Heredia got his visa. He came to America in July—and then had to serve a three-week suspension from Major League Baseball. He went 0-3 for the Indians and was let go after the season. He played four more years, winning just 18 more games—one fewer than that wonderful 2007 season, which turned out to be a flash in the pan.

THE ABRUPT DEPARTURE OF BRAYLON EDWARDS

Braylon Edwards arrived in Cleveland with panache. He left in a hurry.

An All-American wide receiver from the University of Michigan, Edwards was taken third overall by the Browns in the 2005 draft. He showed off his style immediately, wearing a 15-carat diamond bracelet, a diamond-encrusted watch and diamond earrings to his introductory news conference. He also drove a new Bentley. His flair was more fit for, say, Miami, which drafted one spot ahead of Cleveland and took Ronnie Brown. And Edwards was upset at then-Dolphins coach Nick Saban for not picking him.

Edwards held out in training camp, and ended up signing a five-year, $40 million deal, with $18.5 million of it guaranteed. His rookie year left a little to be desired, shortened by a torn ACL. His 2006 year was most notable for the fact that when his alma mater was ranked second and playing first-ranked Ohio State, he rented a helicopter to fly him from Cleveland to Columbus. Coach Romeo Crennel was unamused, benching him for the beginning of the next day's game (an eventual 24-20 loss to Pittsburgh).

But in 2007 he was a Pro Bowler and a big reason the Browns

went 10-6, just missing the playoffs. He had 80 catches for 1,289 yards, including 16 touchdowns. But even then, drops were a problem. His 12 were second in the NFL.

The following year, Edwards, who had to get stitches in training camp after having his ankle stepped on while running without shoes in a foot race, led the NFL in dropped passes, earning the nickname "Edwards Scissorhands." The Browns fell to earth with a thud, going 4-12, and coach Romeo Crennel and general manager Phil Savage were shown the door. In came Eric Mangini, a former Browns ball boy who'd distinguished himself as an assistant for Bill Belichick in New England and briefly as the Jets' head coach.

Mangini demanded total buy-in from players, and said if they didn't buy in, he'd be happy to try to arrange their departure. Edwards had a meeting with the Mangenius, and in an interview with nyjets.com in 2020 recalled telling him, "I've been here four and a half years and I think you're a heck of a nice guy. I just don't think that this is a situation or a team that's conducive to winning right now. I don't know if it's ownership, if it's management, if it's coaching, if it's whatever. This is just a place I need to get out of. So, if you can do anything, I'll be happy."

In what turned out to be his final game as a Brown, Edwards had no catches in a home loss to the Bengals on Oct. 4, 2009 and drew a 15-yard unsportsmanlike conduct penalty after sharing some words with Cincinnati lineman Pat Sims.

That night, Edwards was out at View Ultralounge on Prospect Avenue downtown. Also out that evening was Edward Givens, a promoter and friend of LeBron James, who at the time dominated the Cleveland sports landscape.

"Braylon comes up and started saying things, degrading me," Givens told the *Plain Dealer*. "He said if it wasn't for LeBron or the Four Horsemen [James' friends and business partners], I wouldn't have what I have, nor would I be able to get girls. The conversation started to escalate. As some of his teammates started to pull him back, he punched me."

It was a cardinal sin. You don't cross LeBron James, whom comedian Mike Polk Jr. referred to as the basis of Cleveland's economy in his "Hastily Made Cleveland Tourism Video" on Youtube. The best humor contains some truth.

Two days later, Edwards was gone, traded to the Jets for receiver Chansi Stuckey, linebacker Jason Trusnick and two draft picks in the following year's NFL draft. Edwards was thrilled to be in New York City. The Detroit-area native noted that his New York-type essence led to clashes in Cleveland, where he said there was nothing going on.

Edwards lasted two years with the Jets before he was waived. He was then picked up by the 49ers, coached at the time by Michigan grad and future Wolverines coach Jim Harbaugh. It seemed like a perfect fit for Edwards. In a 2008 *Beacon Journal* interview with Maria Ridenour, he said of his time in Cleveland, "Since Day One I've been a marked man coming from Michigan."

Edwards was waived after one season by the Bay.

THE RISE AND FALL OF PEYTON HILLIS

In March 2010, the Browns traded Brady Quinn to the Broncos. Quinn, a Columbus-area native who'd grown up a Browns fan, had been drafted in the first round three years earlier, but he became just one more name on the infamous Browns quarterback jersey.

The Browns got a couple of draft picks for Quinn—and a one-year wonder and future video game cover boy: Peyton Hillis.

Hillis, an Arkansas native, played college football at the University of Arkansas, where he was overshadowed by Darren McFadden and Felix Jones. It would be a recurring theme in his career: He would go unnoticed until he was needed.

The Broncos took a flyer on him in the seventh round of the 2008 NFL Draft. Ostensibly a fullback, he was pressed into service as a running back—coincidentally, against the Browns on a Thursday night. "I was never the most athletic or the fastest running back," he recalled in an interview with ClevelandBrowns.com. "But I was the biggest."

Once everyone else recovered, though, he was relegated to blocking for the Broncos. But when he came to Cleveland, coach Eric Mangini planned to use him as a running back—and he was the starter by Week 3.

Hillis scored 11 touchdowns and ran for 1,165 yards—just the third Browns running back to gain more than 1,000 yards since the team returned in 1999. (Nicknamed the Albino Rhino, he was also the first white running back in a generation to gain 1,000 yards in a season.) Hillis also caught 61 passes for another 477 yards and two more touchdowns.

That offseason, EA Sports announced that it would let fans vote on who would grace the cover of its 2012 version of the Madden NFL video game.

The Browns—and fans—rallied behind Hillis as their endorsed choice. In the 32-team bracket, he advanced past the Chiefs' Jamaal Charles, Falcons quarterback Matt Ryan, Ravens running back Ray Rice, Packers quarterback (and occasional *Jeopardy!* host) Aaron Rodgers and finally, in the finals, Eagles quarterback Michael Vick, prevailing by a two-to-one margin.

"I've got to give it up to the Cleveland fans," Hillis said in an interview with Cleveland.com's Jodie Valade when he received the honor. "It shows how big Cleveland fans are to the players, and I'm going to try my best for them."

He did a whirlwind tour in New York City, taking the cover photo in Times Square and telling David Letterman the Top 10 perks of being the Madden cover boy—including free back massages from John Madden, being the frontrunner to replace Charlie Sheen on *Two and a Half Men* and a new catchphrase: "Watchoo talkin' 'bout, Hillis?"

But he also had to contend with the infamous Madden curse. Previous Madden cover subjects like Troy Polamalu, Shaun Alexander and Donovan McNabb had strange injuries befall them the next year. Vince Young never reached the heights he had the year before he was on the cover, and Brett Favre got the cover as a retirement present—and then promptly unretired.

But Hillis' fate would be a unique one. It started with the firing of Mangini following the season. It was the second straight year the Browns had gone 5-11, and Randy Lerner handed the keys to the castle over to Mike Holmgren, who no doubt wanted to bring in his own personnel. His choice for head coach was Pat Shurmur, whose main claim to fame at that point was that his uncle Fritz had been Holmgren's defensive coordinator in Green Bay.

Shurmur was installing a West Coast offense, and Hillis had lost his biggest backer in Mangini. The 2011 season would be the last for Hillis on his rookie deal, and the churn in the Browns' front office, as well as a lockout in the NFL, kept him from getting a new contract.

He missed a game, ostensibly due to strep throat, but he'd reported to the stadium, declared himself out and then went home, later saying it was on advice of his agent—one of three he cycled through in 2011.

He had a hamstring injury that kept him out of another game—but he was shown throwing balls on the sideline with third-string quarterback Thad Lewis. Veteran players had to hold an intervention for him. LeCharles Bentley accused him of blowing off a charity function. He had become a distraction—and worse yet, he wasn't contributing at the level he had the previous year.

Hillis was a free agent following the season. The Browns opted to use their franchise tag on kicker Phil Dawson—and didn't even make Hillis an offer. At one point, there was a rumor that Hillis was ready to quit football and join the CIA. He denied that—and managed to play for three more years, one for the Chiefs and two for the Giants. He was like a star, streaking across the sky, shining brightly for a moment before fading.

At least we'll always have the Madden cover.

SPECIAL DELIVERY FOR CHRIS PEREZ

Being a relief pitcher requires a certain kind of personality. You have to be willing to take on high-pressure situations—and then forget them almost instantly if they go sideways on you. You have to be able to throw strikes. It's not typically a finesse job, either.

Indians fans rode the rollercoaster with a litany of closers. There was Jose Mesa, so automatic in 1995, yet responsible for the worst moment in a lot of Tribe fans' memories. There was roly-poly Bob Wickman—briefly supplanted by heat-throwing lunatic John Rocker. There was Joe Borowski, who inspired agita in baseball fans throughout Northeast Ohio, followed by Kerry Wood, who seemed to throw gasoline on the fire rather than put it out.

And then there was Chris Perez, who arrived in Cleveland in June 2009 from the Cardinals as part of the return for Mark DeRosa, a utility player who appeared in 71 games for the Indians after being acquired in the previous off-season. (The deal included a player to be named later for the Indians, who turned out to be Jess Todd.)

Perez was a first-round pick of the Cardinals in the 2006 draft, and made his major league debut two years later, going 3-3 with seven saves for St. Louis. He made 32 appearances in his first half-season in Cleveland, getting one save. Wood was still the closer at that point, but when he was dealt to the Yankees at mid-season the following year, the job became Perez's.

And he rose to the occasion, making 37 appearances in 2010, with 23 saves and a sparkling 1.71 ERA. He also leaned into the lunacy that has to be part of being a good closer. He'd get so worked up in relief appearances that he'd occasionally vomit on the mound.

By then, every closer had a song that played when they came into a game. It was Metallica's "Enter Sandman" for Mariano Rivera. For Jonathan Papelbon of the Red Sox, it was "I'm Shipping Up to Boston" by Dropkick Murphys. Trevor Hoffman of the Padres used "Hell's Bells." Perez's? "Firestarter" by The Prodigy. His nickname and Twitter handle were "Pure Rage."

And he was never shy about interacting with opposing players—or even fans. After ringing up Jarrod Dyson of the Royals, Perez walked off the mound and did the John Cena "you can't see me" hand wave. After another Royals game included a couple of hit batters and emptied benches, he tweeted "You hit us, we hit you. Period," earning a fine from MLB.

He got lip from an Athletics fan in Oakland—and gave it back, profanely. He wasn't above calling out Indians fans either, who weren't showing up to watch the team in 2011, when they got out to a raucous start and were leading the American League Central.

Perez was named to the American League All-Star team in 2011 and 2012. Both years, the Indians started strong, but both years, they faded. They lost 12 of their first 19 after the break in 2011 and finished 80-82. The following year was even worse, as the Indians went 5-24 in August, tying a team record for the most losses in a month, and finished the year 68-94. It was the third time in four years that the Indians had lost more than 90 games. Out went manager Manny Acta—and Perez was happy to see him go, saying his non-confrontational style didn't serve the Indians well as they were in a full-on collapse—and in came Terry Francona.

In 2013, Perez's velocity started to slip, just a couple miles per hour, and he was still throwing in the 90s, but it was enough that it started to make a difference. He had shoulder surgery prior to the season and was placed on the disabled list at the end of May.

On June 4, 2013, a package came to Perez's home in Rocky River. The postal carrier gave the package to Perez's wife Melanie and inquired about the addressee: Brody Baum. Melanie's maiden name was Baum, and the family dog was named Brody. She told the carrier to leave the package on the porch.

The carrier was in reality an undercover postal inspector, from the enforcement and investigation arm of the U.S. Postal Service. When the package, bearing a Los Angeles return address, came to the Rocky River post office, a supervisor noticed it smelled like marijuana. It was also Priority Mail, which was used to ship controlled substances because of its timeliness and traceability.

A drug-sniffing dog was brought in from Cleveland police, and it reacted like the package contained drugs.

Chris and Melanie Perez went out for the afternoon for lunch and a movie, and returned to find law enforcement at their home. The parcel contained a total of 9.65 ounces of marijuana. Melanie Perez suggested that a fan might have sent the package.

Both were charged with misdemeanor marijuana possession, and both were sentenced to probation and ordered to pay fines. But closers have short shelf lives, and Perez's expiration date was at hand. In August, he stopped speaking to the media. He watched the Indians make their first postseason appearance in six years, losing the wild card game at home to the Tampa Bay Rays, and was released after the season.

He latched on with the Dodgers for a year, and signed a minor-league contract with the Brewers, which included a spring training invitation. He didn't make the team and ultimately opted out of the deal. In June, while a free agent, he was hit with a 50-game suspension for violating MLB's drug policy.

He retired that August.

THE SAGA OF JOHNNY FOOTBALL

There was more than a little risk when the Browns drafted Johnny Manziel 22nd overall in 2014.

He was a fun player to watch at Texas A&M, turning busted plays into something exciting, beating Nick Saban's Alabama juggernaut and winning the Heisman Trophy. But even then, there were rumors of substance abuse and immature, if not problematic, behavior. Before he was named the Aggies' starter, he'd gotten into an alcohol-fueled fight while out drinking underage with a fake ID. He'd overslept prior to a kids' football camp, and got rapped on the knuckles by the NCAA for being paid to sign autographs.

"During the draft process, not one person interviewed by the team said he was going to grow up," one source directly involved in drafting Manziel said in an ESPN story after Manziel's rookie year. "You can't blame Johnny. This is who he is. The team knew that."

But in what seems to be a recurring theme with the Browns' front office—whoever it may be—Manziel was believed to be worth the risk. And the investment paid off initially, as his selection was met with a spike in merchandise and season ticket sales. Manziel did nothing to dispel their concerns, though, when photos surfaced of him in June drinking champagne from the bottle on an inflatable swan in a pool at an X-Games party. Video also surfaced that month of him talking into a stack of cash, saying, "I can't hear you, there's too much fucking money in my hand!"

Mike Pettine, himself a rookie head coach, was determined to bring Manziel along slowly—and Manziel certainly did his part by failing to light the world on fire during training camp. His most notable preseason moment came when he gave the Washington Redskins a one-fingered salute during an exhibition game.

The starting quarterback for the opener that year would be Brian Hoyer, a North Olmsted native and St. Ignatius grad who was returning from a repaired ACL.

"This being the Browns, I think everyone thought Hoyer would come out and lose the first three games, and they'd have to put in Johnny," recalled Daryl Ruiter of 92.3 The Fan for a lengthy *Vanity Fair* feature on Manziel.

But the Browns can't even Browns correctly. They came out and started winning, a testament to offensive coordinator Kyle Shanahan playing to Hoyer's strengths, and a stout offensive line. But starting center Alex Mack broke his leg, and Hoyer reached his ceiling as the Browns, leading the division in November, had fallen back to the pack. The time had come for Johnny Cleveland to make his debut, starting against the Bengals at home in a game the Browns very much needed to win to stay in the playoff hunt.

It was an unmitigated disaster, with the Browns losing 30-0. Manziel had 80 yards passing, two interceptions and a QBR of 1.0. The Browns finished the season 7-9, with Manziel on injured reserve. He was scheduled for a medical appointment the day before the Browns' finale, but overslept, allegedly after having too much fun the night before.

Following the season, Manziel said all the right things, and reiterated his commitment to football. He then went on a whirlwind tour that included Miami (where he wished LeBron James a happy 30th birthday via Instagram), Houston (where he had a drink thrown on him in a club) and Aspen. That February, he checked himself into a rehabilitation program for substance abuse. He'd moved out of The 9, a hotel/apartment complex on East Ninth Street downtown, for a more bucolic environment—a large house on a golf course (probably his second favorite sport) in Avon.

Brian Hoyer left in free agency, and the Browns signed quarterback Josh McCown, who was named the starter, and would serve as a mentor to Manziel. But McCown tried to dive into the end zone in the season opener against the Jets, was hit, helicoptered and fumbled into the end zone. He was put into the league's concussion protocol, and Manziel got the start week 2 against the Titans. He got his first win as a starting quarterback that week, but McCown was suitably recovered and was named the starter for week 3.

The move, Manziel's friends said, started a spiral for him. In October, police pulled over a white Nissan in Avon. It was a rolling domestic dispute between Manziel and his girlfriend Colleen Crowley. He was drinking again. But then in week 7 McCown sustained a shoulder injury, and Pettine said Manziel would be the starter for the rest of the season.

"I'm not going to do anything that's going to be a distraction to this team or be an embarrassment to the organization," Manziel said, before leaving town for the bye week, in a statement released to media by the team.

Then video surfaced of Manziel partying in Texas. At first, he feebly attempted an explanation, saying the video was shot months earlier and only now was going viral. But he eventually came clean, and Pettine started third-string quarterback Austin Davis against the Ravens in a game that turned out to be memorable to Browns fans for all the wrong reasons.

The Austin Davis experience was a disaster. Josh McCown was still injured. Pettine had no choice but to return to Manziel as the starting quarterback. He led a win over the 49ers, but the Browns lost their next two. Going into the season finale against Pittsburgh, Manziel appeared disheveled—and possibly inebriated—in a team meeting. He claimed he had concussion symptoms, and was put into the league's protocol. He wouldn't be active for the Browns' season finale against the Steelers.

Following the team walk-through Saturday morning, Manziel hopped on a plane—wearing a hoodie and dark glasses so he wouldn't be recognized—and headed to Las Vegas. Even by the terrible standards of Johnny Manziel's decision making, this was one bad choice after another. He sent a photo out on his Instagram of him and his dog, with a tag that he was in Avon, Ohio, while he was out in Vegas. He saw a Chainsmokers concert. He went to dinner. He bought a blonde wig and fake mustache and was seen at gaming tables. By the time he returned to his hotel room, it was an hour before he was scheduled to be in Cleveland before the game.

"'I'm definitely not going to make that,'" Manziel said in a 2018 podcast with Joe Thomas and Andrew Hawkins. "I just turn my phone off and throw it in the drawer and I'm like, 'We'll figure it out when we wake up.'"

The season ended with a loss. Pettine and general manager Ray Farmer were both fired. Hue Jackson was hired as coach, and nobody had any patience left for Johnny Manziel. He was cut as soon as the league year started in March.

Manziel had allegedly told a Browns assistant he wanted to "wreck this league." He ended up wrecking a lot of things along the way.

MYCHAL KENDRICKS' INSIDER TRADING

The Browns signed Mychal Kendricks in 2018, getting a talented linebacker who was part of the Eagles' Super Bowl-winning team. But Kendricks, who was thwarted in demands for a trade the season before, had to undergo ankle surgery in March, a month after the Super Bowl win, and became a salary cap casualty in Philadelphia.

His arrival in Cleveland was mysterious in and of itself, with denials at a deal being done right up until the signing was announced. It was seen as a move that not only added depth to the team's linebacking corps but put him in the mix to start immediately.

"Kendricks will start from day one for Cleveland," journalist and podcaster Jordan Schulz wrote on Twitter.

But by the time the regular season rolled around, Kendricks wasn't even on the team.

On Aug. 29, 2018, a federal attorney in Philadelphia announced that Kendricks had been charged with insider trading. An investigation alleged that Kendricks made investments using illegal insider information from a bank analyst, whom he'd repaid with money, Eagles tickets and other perks.

Kendricks offered a blanket apology to fans, the Eagles and Browns and his family, saying in a statement released by the team, "You all deserve better, and I will work my hardest to re-earn your trust and respect, serve as an advocate to educate others, and show you that I will never be involved in anything like this again. Thank you for your time and hopefully your forgiveness."

Within hours, the Browns had released him.

His involvement with an insider trading investigation was not news to Browns management (nor to the Eagles, who were aware of it when it started—and when he became a free agent earlier that year). But his indictment was news to Browns General Manager John Dorsey.

"We were told Mychal had fully cooperated with investigators as a victim," he said in a statement released to the media. "From what was communicated at that time and based on the numerous questions we asked and further due diligence on our part, including checking with the league office, there was no information discovered that conveyed otherwise.

"Recently, we were provided an update on the matter and the circumstances have changed. We are now dealing with a different set of facts and the additional information we've gathered has led us to the decision to release Mychal from our team."

Kendricks quickly found a home in Seattle—but first came an eight-game suspension for violating the NFL's personal conduct policy. He pleaded guilty to insider trading, and was sentenced to a day in jail, three years' probation and 300 hours of community service, in addition to a fine and restitution.

GREG ROBINSON'S ENORMOUS POT BUST

When Greg Robinson arrived at Auburn, he was one of the most highly touted offensive line prospects in America. Prior to being taken second overall by the then-St. Louis Rams in the 2014 NFL Draft, scouts believed he had Hall of Fame potential.

But by the time he got to the Browns in 2018, he was an unwanted free agent on his way to being one of the biggest draft busts (non-Browns division) in recent memory. And by the time he left two years later, he was facing federal drug charges.

Robinson was signed to a one-year contract initially to add depth to an offensive line that recently had been a team strength but was becoming more patchwork by the day. Joe Thomas had missed the last nine games of the 2017 season with a torn bicep, and then opted to retire, leading to a brief preseason experiment of Joel Bitonio at left tackle. Donald Stephenson would start the season suspended, and rookie Austin Corbett wasn't impressing anyone at training camp.

Since Robinson didn't have the high expectations (or high salary) he did in St. Louis, the bar was lower for him in Cleveland. (Of course, Robinson also probably benefitted from the fact that the Browns had gone 1-31 in the preceding two years and were looking for anyone with a pulse that could perform like an actual NFL player.) He played all 16 games that season, and after Hue Jackson was fired, replaced Desmond Harrison as the starting left tackle for the season's final eight games. (Harrison would gain his own infamy the following year, when he was released after missing a flight to Browns minicamp.) That year, the Browns went 7-8-1, by far their best season in years. The Browns re-signed him to another one-year deal, then surprisingly cut him in early September right before the season started.

But it was a procedural shuffling to keep other players under contract and on the active roster, and Robinson was quickly brought back into the fold. Robinson was thrown out of the Browns' opener for kicking a Titans player. The Browns were drubbed, and they—not Robinson—wilted under high expectations, finishing the season 6-10. One of the ongoing issues was the offensive line, and a more permanent solution than Robinson was needed.

In February 2020—not long before the new NFL year started—news broke that Robinson was facing federal charges of marijuana possession. Robinson and Quan Bray, a teammate of his at Auburn who had briefly played in the NFL, had rented a sport-utility vehicle in Los Angeles, and the two of them, along with an Uber driver they'd met the year before, were driving the Chevrolet Tahoe to Louisiana.

The Tahoe was stopped at a border patrol checkpoint near El Paso, Texas, and searched after a drug-sniffing dog reacted to the vehicle. Inside, they found duffel bags containing a total of 157 pounds of marijuana. According to a criminal complaint, Robinson and Bray tried to get the Uber driver—the only one of the three who wasn't charged in the incident—to take the rap. Robinson and Bray were ultimately charged with conspiracy to possess marijuana with intent to deliver.

Robinson had already been informed by the Browns that he would not be re-signed. (The Browns would end up drafting Alabama tackle Jedrick Wills in the first round that spring.) The arrest did nothing to raise his free agent stock.

JERMAINE WHITEHEAD TAKES TO TWITTER

The Browns snagged defensive back Jermaine Whitehead off waivers in November 2018. He was available after being released by the Packers following his ejection from a Sunday night game for slapping David Andrews.

That should have been a hint right there.

He was picked up by interim coach Gregg Williams, himself a, uh, let's say passionate man. The Browns tendered Whitehead an offer the following March—by which time Williams had moved on. Freddie Kitchens had been named head coach and assembled a staff, including defensive coordinator Steve Wilks, who said in a news conference, "Jermaine Whitehead is a leader in my opinion."

Used exclusively on special teams in his first season with the Browns, Whitehead became a key part of the Browns secondary in 2019. "I have a lot of confidence in Jermaine," Kitchens said in a news conference at the end of October. It was misplaced.

In a game against the Broncos on Nov. 3, Denver quarterback Brandon Allen threw to tight end Noah Fant, who was running a slant route. Fant took a glancing blow from Whitehead and ran for a 75-yard touchdown. The Broncos ended up winning the game 24-19.

In social media and on the radio, analyst Dustin Fox criticized Whitehead, tweeting that his tackling effort that day was a joke. After the game—still in uniform—Whitehead took to Twitter, telling Fox, "Come get it in blood bitch made ass lil boy. I'm out there with a broke hand . . . don't get smoked fuck ass cracker." He threatened to kill at least one other fan, and his Twitter account was suspended briefly. But when it returned, he was still as com-bative, saying, "any of these hatin ass crackers can come catch these hands."

As expected, the Browns' reaction was swift, releasing a state-ment that night. "Jermaine Whitehead's social media posts follow-ing today's game were totally unacceptable and highly inappro-priate," Browns spokesman Andrew Gribble said in a statement on Twitter. "We immediately spoke with Jermaine upon learning of these comments. The Browns in no way condone that type of language or behavior. This matter will be further addressed inter-nally."

The following day, he was gone. He returned to social media, offering apologies on Instagram, but he hasn't played for an NFL team since.

LARCENY INC.

Stealing is encouraged in sports. In baseball, bases are stolen. Steals are tracked in basketball as well. And one of the all-important stats in football is the takeaway. But sometimes, thievery goes beyond the field of play.

JASON GRIMSLEY'S MISSION IMPOSSIBLE

After decades as a punchline, the Indians were finally starting to show some punch of their own in 1994. The move into Jacobs Field combined with the blossoming of a team that suddenly had offensive firepower to spare.

A large part of that offensive output was Albert Belle. The Indians drafted Belle in the second round of the 1987 draft. He made his debut as Joey Belle—his given name is Albert Jojuan Belle—two years later. Following a stint for alcohol rehabilitation, he re-emerged as Albert Belle, becoming known almost as much for his truculence as for his prodigious hitting. And there was suspicion that while his anger came naturally, his hitting might have received some aid.

In 1994, the American and National leagues realigned into three divisions. Where there had been East and West Divisions since 1969, now there were East, West and Central divisions. The White Sox were in full ascent, having won the West Division the year before, but the Indians were neck and neck, tied for first in the new

Central Division as they came to Chicago for their first series out of the All-Star Break. Belle homered in the first game, a 6-3 White Sox win, and when he came up to the plate in the first inning of the second game with one on, one out and the Indians holding a 1-0 lead, White Sox manager Gene Lamont engaged in a bit of gamesmanship.

Lamont challenged Belle's bat as being illegal, a not-uncommon gambit that came up from time to time in baseball (famously when Billy Martin said George Brett's bat had too much pine tar on it in a 1983 Yankees-Royals matchup that's become known as the Pine Tar Game). Lamont alleged that Belle used a corked bat, also not necessarily uncommon. Baseball bats are required to be made from solid wood. Theoretically, a bat that's been "corked"— hollowed out inside and the wood replaced with cork—would be lighter, thus enabling the hitter to get a higher bat speed.

The science is up for debate, but Belle surrendered the bat to umpire Dave Phillips and it was taken to the umpire's locker room for safekeeping.

Belle mumbled "that's bullshit" before getting another bat and grounding into a fielder's choice, but it was a corked bat. In fact, *all* of Belle's bats were corked, as later recounted in Omar Vizquel's autobiography. A potential suspension of Belle could be a body blow in a heated pennant race.

Indians pitcher Jason Grimsley saw a solution. "As I was sitting there," Grimsley recalled in 1999 to the *New York Times*, "the thought came to my mind: I can get that bat."

Grimsley disappeared into the clubhouse, which had a drop ceiling throughout it. Grabbing a flashlight, he climbed into the ceiling from manager Mike Hargrove's desk and then crawled along the tops of the cinder block walls that separated one locker room from another. After about a 30-minute odyssey shimmying through the clubhouse ceilings with a replacement bat and a flashlight, he came to the umpires' dressing room. He switched Belle's bat with one belonging to first baseman Paul Sorrento, then returned quickly to the dugout to watch the remainder of the Indians' 3-2 win over the White Sox.

Almost immediately, it was apparent that the perfect crime hadn't been committed. Belle's confiscated bat had been virtually brand-new. Sorrento's showed significant signs of use. Bits of insulation found on the floor indicated the ceiling tiles had been moved.

MLB head of security Kevin Hallinan, who had previously worked as an FBI agent investigating organized crime, came to Chicago, and the umpires' locker room was dusted for prints. "This is bizarre," American League Supervisor of Umpires Marty Springstead said in the *Chicago Tribune*. "In 31 years, you think you've seen it all but you haven't."

Ultimately, amnesty was offered. The offending bat was returned, and Belle was given a 10-game suspension (reduced to seven on appeal). The crime was officially unsolved until Grimsley revealed his role in the interview in 1999, by which time he played with the Yankees. "That was one of the biggest adrenaline rushes I've ever experienced," he said.

CRIME, PUNISHMENT AND O. J.

For those of a certain age, there was no more All-American figure than O. J. Simpson. After a Heisman Trophy-winning career at Southern California, Simpson was the first choice in the first common AFL-NFL draft. He became the first NFL running back to gain 2,000 yards in a season, and by the time he retired, he'd virtually rewritten the NFL record book. In 1985, he was inducted into the Pro Football Hall of Fame in Canton, in the first year he was eligible. He was also a personable, charismatic figure, ripe for the screen. He ran through airports for Hertz in commercials, rescued a kitten in *The Towering Inferno*, and clowned around as Leslie Nielsen's inept but well-meaning partner in the *Naked Gun* movies.

That all changed on June 12, 1994, when Simpson's ex-wife Nicole Brown Simpson and her friend Ronald Goldman were found brutally murdered at her home in Brentwood, California, a suburb of Los Angeles. Simpson was immediately regarded as a "person of interest," and five days later, with his friend Al Cowlings driving a white Ford Bronco, led police on a slow-speed chase through Los Angeles. Simpson was charged and his trial began the following January.

On July 23, 1995 in Canton, festivities were beginning at the Pro Football Hall of Fame. It was Kickoff Sunday, the start of the annual Hall of Fame week, culminating the following Saturday with inductions and the annual Hall of Fame Game (that year between the NFL's two newest teams, the Jacksonville Jaguars and Carolina Panthers). The hall was crowded, and a construction project was going on. It was a busy day during a busy time. Then, around 5:30 p.m., someone alerted Hall security: Simpson's bust had been stolen.

It was the first time in the hall's history that a bust of an inductee had been stolen. Bronze and weighing around 35 pounds, the busts didn't have the resale value that some of the other memorabilia might, and while other memorabilia had more security measures on them, the busts weren't secured to their displays. It appears someone picked up O. J.'s head, put it in a duffel bag, and just walked out a back door.

"The value of the statue is negligible," hall director Pete Elliott told the Associated Press at the time. "It couldn't really be sold or anything."

The following day, an Ohio Department of Transportation litter crew found the bust, undamaged, near the East 30th Street exit from Interstate 77, not far from downtown Cleveland. The bust was dusted for fingerprints and returned to its spot in the Hall of Fame, this time bolted down, along with the statues commemorating all the other inductees.

Later that year, O. J. was acquitted of the murders (although a later civil suit found him liable and ordered him to pay damages). He said after the criminal trial that he'd find the real killers. The case of who stole O. J.'s bust—the only such theft in the Hall of Fame's history—is similarly unsolved.

AUSTIN CARR'S BANNER STOLEN

It's only right that Austin Carr's name is in the rafters at Rocket Mortgage FieldHouse.

Following an accomplished career at Notre Dame (a half-century later, he remains the school's leading scorer), Carr was drafted first overall by the Cavaliers in 1971 and spent the bulk of his 11-year career wearing the wine and gold. Following his playing days, he joined the Cavs' broadcast team and front office, serving as the team's director of community relations. Even today, he's known as Mr. Cavalier.

On Jan. 27, 2014, professional wrestling's *Monday Night Raw* took place at what was then Quicken Loans Arena. Carr's retired number 34 fluttered in the rafters, beside other honored Cavs alumni including Nate Thurmond and Bingo Smith—teammates of Carr's at the Miracle at Richfield—and broadcaster Joe Tait.

The following day, the Cavs were playing the New Orleans Pelicans. Associated Press workhorse Tom Withers noticed Carr's banner was absent and asked the man himself about it. "I'm coming out of retirement," Carr joked. But the banner was missing, and the Cavs didn't know why. A replacement was quickly hung in the arena rafters, but who stole it, as with O. J.'s bust, remains a mystery.

COACHING AIN'T EASY

When in doubt, the old saw goes, fire the manager.

The coach of a team is in charge of 15 (basketball) to 53 (football) players, arranging complementary talents and managing personalities. Casey Stengel said the key to being a good manager is keeping the players who hate you away from the players who haven't made up their minds.

It doesn't take much to throw off the delicate balance: Capricious, meddling owners; moody, malcontented players; and sometimes, yes, the manager's own ineptitude. Here are some tales of coaching stints that have gone hopelessly and sometimes hilariously off the rails.

THE CURSE OF BOBBY BRAGAN

If you're a Cleveland baseball fan, you've heard of the Curse of Rocky Colavito. Heck, Terry Pluto wrote a book about it. Basically, after the Indians—specifically, their general manager, Frank Lane, for whom doing deals was almost a pathological need—traded fan-favorite outfielder Rocky Colavito just days before the start of the 1960 season to the Tigers, the Tribe wandered the desert for decades, fumbling from one screw-up to the next until finally righting the ship in a new ballpark in the 1990s.

But have you heard of the Curse of Bobby Bragan?

Bragan was a baseball lifer—literally. His last appearance as a manager came at the age of 87 (as did his last ejection as a manager). He had spent most of his playing career as a back-up catcher, then moved to the dugout, being named manager of the Pittsburgh Pirates in 1956. He finished out that season but was fired in August of the following year. He was hired to be the Indians' manager in 1958. There, he became a victim of circumstance. He was hired by Hank Greenberg, the general manager and part owner of the Indians, who was trying to negotiate a move for the franchise to Minneapolis. Greenberg was unsuccessful, and thrown over the side in November as GM, replaced by . . . Frank Lane. (*Of course* Frank Lane has something to do with this curse too, right?)

Seventy-three days into the 1958 season, Bragan was summoned to meet with Lane after a loss to the Red Sox. He relates the conversation in his autobiography: "Bobby," Bragan says Lane told him, "I don't know how we're going to get along without you, but starting tomorrow, we're going to try."

Bragan's 67 games (he finished with a record of 31-36) at the helm of the Tribe remains the shortest stint by any non-interim manager in team history. Shortly after that, the story goes, Bragan hired a witch to put a hex on the team.

Bragan, of course, denied it. "The whole thing was a figment of some disc jockey's imagination," he is quoted as saying in *The Cleveland Indians Encyclopedia*. "The guy asked me how I felt after I was fired, and I told him I felt like putting a curse on the entire organization. I was only joking, but [the disc jockey] thought I was serious or knew it would make a good story."

The Indians entered what could charitably be called a fallow period shortly thereafter. They finished second in 1959, and Lane then wheeled and dealed the Indians into the bottom half of the American League.

"I didn't put a hex on the club," Bragan wrote in his autobiography. "Having Frank Lane as the general manager was curse enough."

In 1984, a traffic helicopter from a local radio station flew over Cleveland Stadium carrying a witch named Elizabeth, who "lifted" the curse. The Indians finished fourth that year—and then lost 102 games the next year, tying a team mark for futility. The record only stood until 1991, when the Indians lost 105 games. (They also lost 101 in 1987, the year of the famed "Indian Uprising" *Sports Illustrated* cover.)

For the team's fortunes to really change, they would need a change of address. Maybe it *was* a hex.

END OF THE LINE FOR COACH SAM

On Oct. 22, 1984, the Browns fired their head coach the day after a 12-9 loss to the Bengals.

That's not an unusual occurrence. Coaches get fired all the time—especially coaches wearing brown and orange. But the coach fired this time was Sam Rutigliano—who then took the unusual step of appearing at the news conference to announce his own firing.

Photos in the next day's *Plain Dealer* showed a table at Cleveland Stadium with Browns owner Art Modell sitting shoulder-to-shoulder with defensive coordinator Marty Schottenheimer, who would take over as head coach, and a stone-faced Rutigliano.

Rutigliano (who had been classmates with future Raiders coach Al Davis at Erasmus High School in Brooklyn) had coached at the high school, college and pro level before being named Browns head coach in 1978, the first coach in the team's history at that point hired from outside the organization. He succeeded Forrest Gregg, whose tenure ended with one game left in the 1977 season with his firing or resignation, depending on who you asked.

Rutigliano went on to coach the Kardiac Kids teams of the late 1970s and early 1980s. The Browns won the AFC Central Division in 1980, led by NFL MVP Brian Sipe. That team's playoff odyssey ended with a late interception to seal a Raiders win on a play that remains known as Red Right 88. Rutigliano was named coach of the year by United Press International in 1979 and 1980.

In 1983, the Browns went 9-7 and failed to make the playoffs. In 1984, they dropped their first three games before beating the Steelers, and then lost the next three, precipitating Rutigliano's firing—the first Browns coach to be fired midseason. Modell said it was a difficult decision, but one he felt he had to make. Players found out about the firing when they heard it on the radio. Modell planned to honor the remainder of Rutigliano's contract, which had been extended just months earlier. Schottenheimer talked about taking on offensive duties as the new head coach.

Rutigliano, for his part, tried to be a company man, saying he was going from coach to the team's number one fan, but the one-liners he was known for had lost their bite—and their audience.

"My only advice to Marty is to make sure you kick field goals," Rutigliano told the *Plain Dealer*, referring to a recent close loss to the Patriots—and probably a little to Red Right 88. (To this day, fans still wonder why the pass play was called, rather than a field goal attempt.)

It was Rutigliano's valediction, wrote Tony Grossi in the next day's *Plain Dealer*. "Rutigliano then walked out of the news conference, brushing past a columnist who offered condolences, to the stadium elevator. As the elevator doors closed, the bottom dropped out of Rutigliano's career in Cleveland."

Rutigliano never coached again in the NFL after six and a half years on the Browns' sideline. No Browns head coach since has equaled the length of that tenure.

"They've fired so many guys," Rutigliano said years later in the *Lorain Morning Journal*, "people actually think I'm a good coach."

THE RISE AND FALL OF KEVIN MACKEY

Kevin Mackey was never riding higher than he was on July 11, 1990. That day, Cleveland State University announced a two-year extension of his contract as men's basketball head coach. In the preceding eight seasons, his teams had gone 144-67, most notably 29-4 in 1985–86, including beating Bobby Knight and Indiana University to advance to the Sweet 16 of the NCAA Tournament before falling to "The Admiral," David Robinson and Navy.

Mackey was a Boston native and former Boston College assistant coach, renowned for his gritty background and his ability to recruit inner-city players. The success Cleveland State had attained on his watch was unsurpassed in the school's brief history—so much so that a new arena was being built on the college's campus, on the eastern edge of downtown. "The House that Kevin Built," it was nicknamed, for the guy who was sometimes called the King of Cleveland.

"It's great to be out of jail," Mackey said in the next day's *Plain Dealer*, referring to NCAA sanctions on CSU for recruiting violations, including a two-year postseason ban. But his words became ironic two days later when Mackey was arrested after emerging from an east side drug house with a woman who most certainly was not his wife. TV news crews filmed him being pulled over in his Lincoln Town Car and arrested.

A week later, Mackey was fired. It was revealed that he'd been leading a double life. He had a girlfriend—and a drug problem.

"I just said that I fired Kevin Mackey, but really, he fired himself," university President John A. Flower said at a news conference that was carried live on Cleveland TV. "It has become clear over the past few days that Kevin Mackey has, by his own admission, habitually and repeatedly made a mockery of standards of moral and ethical behavior."

Mackey pleaded no contest to charges of drug abuse and DUI. His marriage ended, following revelations of his affairs and the fact that he had forged his wife's signature on a credit application. He made the obligatory penitent news conference appearance, and went to a rehabilitation center run by former NBA player John Lucas. Later, Mackey bounced around basketball's minor leagues—at one point coaching for a team owned by former Cavs owner Ted Stepien in Mansfield, Ohio—until 2002, when he joined the Indiana Pacers as a scout. (Team president Larry Bird remembered Mackey from when they were in Boston together, Bird with the Celtics and Mackey as an assistant at Boston College).

Cleveland State's new arena opened in 1991. It's now known as the Wolstein Center. Nobody calls it the House that Kevin Built.

"HE GOT TO MAKE ALL HIS MISTAKES HERE"

On Feb. 5, 1991, the Browns announced their newest head coach. Introducing new coaches had become a habit in Cleveland. After Sam Rutigliano's firing, Marty Schottenheimer lasted for a little over four years before he and Art Modell parted ways—down to having competing news conferences. The Browns got bad in a hurry under Marty's successor, Bud Carson, falling to a 3-13 record in 1990, at the time the worst record in Browns history. (Those were the days . . .)

But the next new head coach the Browns hired had an impressive pedigree, even though he was the youngest head coach in the NFL. His father, Steve, a native of the Youngstown area, was a Browns fan and a coach at Hiram College, where young Bill Belichick watched the Browns at training camp. Bill learned about football from his father, and after graduating from Wesleyan University, where he played lacrosse and squash in addition to football, Bill Belichick took a job breaking down film for the Baltimore Colts.

After brief stints as an assistant with the Detroit Lions and

Denver Broncos, Belichick joined Giants coach Ray Perkins' staff. When Perkins left for the daunting task of succeeding Bear Bryant at the University of Alabama, new Giants head coach Bill Parcells kept Belichick. He was defensive coordinator on the Giants' two Super Bowl-winning teams of that era, taking the Browns job little more than a week after the Giants beat the Buffalo Bills in Super Bowl XXV.

Because of that pedigree, and perhaps because he'd been quick on the draw to fire each of his last three head coaches, Browns owner Art Modell gave Belichick a five-year contract. "I wanted to make a statement of confidence in Bill despite his age," Modell said at the introductory news conference. "I also wanted to make a statement as it relates to continuity and stability. I thought it was appropriate to start fresh and give him as much visible support going in as I possibly can."

Belichick's tenure, though, was fraught with problems. He acquired the reputation—maybe not entirely deserved—as a dour, humorless tactician. Players openly mocked his instructions not to talk to media. And he became known as the man who cut local hero Bernie Kosar. But in 1994, under Bill Belichick, the Browns put it together, winning 11 games and advancing to the playoffs as a wild card, where they beat Parcells, then head coach of the New England Patriots, before losing to the Steelers. (It would be the last Browns playoff win for more than a quarter century.)

Expectations were high the following year, with some even calling the Browns a trendy Super Bowl pick. The Browns started the 1995 season 3-1 but fell back to the pack, losing four of their next five. After a loss to the Oilers, rumors that had been swirling for the previous week were officially confirmed: The team would relocate to Baltimore following the season. The bottom fell out for the Browns, who won just once more before the end of the season, with Belichick drawing fire meant for Modell.

After the move to Baltimore was formally approved by NFL owners, Modell repaid Belichick by firing him, saying he wanted to make a clean break with Cleveland. He then hired Baltimore retread Ted Marchibroda as the first coach of the team now known as the Ravens.

Of course, you know the rest of the story. Belichick got another crack at a head coaching job. It could have been with Cleveland. Kosar says he told Al Lerner, owner of the new Cleveland Browns, and team president Carmen Policy to at least consider Belichick as the new head coach. "They laughed at me," Kosar recalled on Tony Rizzo's radio show.

By then, Belichick had returned to his old mentor Parcells and the Meadowlands, this time in Jets green instead of Giants blue. Following the 1999 season, Parcells stepped down as Jets head coach, and Belichick was announced as his successor. But at what was supposed to be his introductory news conference, Belichick scribbled his resignation on a napkin, writing, "I resign as HC of the NYJ." He then became head coach of the Patriots. There, Belichick went on to achieve success unparalleled in the modern NFL, including 17 straight seasons of at least 10 wins and six Super Bowl wins in nine appearances.

"He got to make all his mistakes here," longtime Browns beat writer Mary Kay Cabot told David Halberstam for his book *The Education of a Coach*. "And to learn from them there."

BUTCH'S PANIC ATTACK

In what was becoming a recurring theme, Browns fans thought the team had hit it out of the park with another coaching hire in 2001. Chris Palmer had shepherded the expansion Browns through their first two seasons, going 5-27. The next hire was a splashy one: owner Al Lerner and team president Carmen Policy went into the college ranks and hired Butch Davis from the University of Miami.

Davis was a protégé of Jimmy Johnson, having served as an assistant to him at Oklahoma State, the University of Miami and with the Dallas Cowboys. Davis had returned to Miami, winning three Big East titles and recruiting a boatload of future NFL talent. The hope was that he could do the same thing in Cleveland that his mentor Johnson had done in Dallas: turn a team from a laughing-stock into a powerhouse.

Lerner introduced him as "the best example I've ever seen of the complete package," according to the *Plain Dealer*.

And it seemed like Davis was on the right path. The Browns improved to 7-9 in 2001, winning more games than they had in the previous two seasons combined. The following year, the Browns went 9-7 and secured a playoff appearance on the last day of the season. In the AFC wild card game, at Heinz Field, the Browns led the Steelers by 17 points but ended up losing. A dropped pass by wide receiver Dennis Northcutt that would have gone for a first down, salting away the Browns' first road playoff win since 1969, has entered the pantheon of Browns heartbreak. But Bruce Arians, who was offensive coordinator at the time, says blame for the loss should rest with Davis. "Our head coach lost the game," he said in an interview eight years later for NBC Sports's Pro Football Talk (ironically, while the Steelers' offensive coordinator). "He called off the dogs on defense."

Davis had assumed total control of personnel on the field and in the front office, effectively forcing out director of football personnel Dwight Clark, who resigned before the 2002 season. But uneasy is the head that wears the crown. Al Lerner died during the 2002 season, and his son Randy inherited the team. Al had envisioned a 10-year plan; Randy was not as patient—and told Davis to cut salary. Among the casualties was the team's first draft pick, quarterback Tim Couch.

Despite Lerner's ultimatum, Davis was given a three-year extension before the 2004 season, reporting directly to Lerner. (That move ran off former Packers GM Ron Wolf, who'd been hired as a consultant.) Davis now had the keys to the castle, but with the team at 3-7 leading into a game against the Bengals on Nov. 28, mired in a four-game losing streak, talk was that Davis was a dead man walking. "It's like a funeral parlor," a source told Tony Grossi, then of the *Plain Dealer*. Davis said he had no plans to resign; the Browns said they had no plans to fire him.

Then, suddenly, Davis was out—resigning following a 58-48 loss to the Bengals. Afterward, Davis said he'd had a panic attack the morning of the game, telling *Sports Illustrated* that the pressure to win had become suffocating. Local media noted that Davis' departure came as the team was the worst it had ever been on his watch and management was contemplating hiring a general manager to oversee personnel. (Davis' draft picks—like those of pretty much everyone who's made them for the Browns—could be charitably described as checkered. In three drafts, he picked 23 players. None made a Pro Bowl.)

"His failures had begun to eclipse even the colossal failure of his team," a *Plain Dealer* editorial said. "His legacy, in a word, is awful." In at least one respect, that proved wrong. Things would get even worse—bad enough that Davis' regime would one day seem like the good old days.

HUE JACKSON JUMPS INTO LAKE ERIE

OK, stop me if you've heard this one before: It's 2016, and the Browns have fired yet another head coach. But this time, the hire is absolutely going to be the right guy. (And if you believe that, I've got some beachfront property in Akron to sell you.)

This time, the outgoing head coach was Mike Pettine, who had been hired just two years earlier after an exhaustive search. That search had been exhaustive mostly because the *previous* head coach, Rob Chudzinski, had been thrown over the side after just one year at the helm, and as a result everyone else the Browns wanted to hire wanted no part of the job. Pettine was the third coach fired by Browns owner Jimmy Haslam, who, after buying the team in 2012, had demonstrated a hair trigger concerning personnel moves.

This time, they'd get it right. Unlike every head coaching hire Haslam had made to that point—and all but two previous head coach hires in the Browns' history tracing back to their founding in 1946—the team hired someone who'd previously been an NFL head coach. They scored a major coup, snapping up Hue Jackson, who was the in-demand coach that offseason. In his lone year at the helm of the Raiders, Hue Jackson had gone 8-8, but his firing came after the team changed general managers. Surely, he was just collateral damage, right? A victim of circumstance?

"He is smart," owner Jimmy Haslam said at Jackson's introductory news conference. "He is tough. He is confident. He is competitive. He has been a head coach before. He has a great offensive mind. He has a tremendous track record developing quarterbacks."

"If I didn't think that we had a chance to do something special here, I wouldn't be here," Jackson said.

What the Browns did under Hue Jackson was historic. But I'm not sure I'd call it special.

To that point, the Detroit Lions were the only team to go winless in a 16-game season, in 2008. It's difficult to go an entire season without winning a game—for the same reason it's difficult for teams to go undefeated in the NFL. Somewhere along the line, one team wins a game it has no business winning, and another loses a game it has no business losing.

In 2016, the Browns seemed determined to lose 'em all—most by double digits, but a few close ones too, like when Cody Parkey shanked a potential game-winning field goal against the Dolphins and the Browns went on to lose in overtime.

Finally, the Browns won one, beating the Chargers on Christmas Eve, their 20-17 win preserved by one missed field goal by Josh Lambo as time expired. (It had been preceded by another attempt nearly four minutes earlier that was blocked by local hero Jamie Meder, who was dubbed the Pierogi Prince of Parma by Joe Thomas.) The win snapped a 17-game losing streak dating back to the 2015 season.

The following week, the Browns lost to the playoff-bound

Steelers' back-ups to close out a 1-15 season, worse even than the Browns' expansion year of 1999.

Yet Browns fans everywhere were oddly relieved. Clearly, they'd bottomed out, right?

Better days had to be ahead, right? Jackson surely thought so. "I'm not going 1-15," Jackson told Pat McManamon of ESPN.com the day after the 2016 season ended. "No. I'll be swimming in that lake over there somewhere. That's not happening."

Better days were not, in fact, ahead. The 2017 season was even worse. The Browns stumbled from one loss to the next, week in and week out. In October, Browns kicker Zane Gonzalez and Titans kicker Ryan Succop traded field goals, with Succop hitting one more in overtime for a 12-9 Titans win.

In December, the Browns held a 21-7 lead on the Packers. They lost that one in overtime too. And there would be no Christmas miracle, with a 20-3 loss on Christmas Eve to the Bears. The Browns headed into the season finale, once again against a Steelers team resting their starters. Of course, they lost.

Hue Jackson was right about one thing: The Browns didn't go 1-15 in 2017. They went 0-16, just the second time in NFL history that a team had gone winless in a 16-game season. Even more ignominious, the Browns became the only team in NFL history to lose 17 straight games, win one to break that streak, and then go on to lose 17 more.

To his credit, Jackson kept his word. On June 1, 2018, joined by about 30 Browns employees, he waded into Lake Erie. It was a warm late spring day, but the lake remained chilly, with water temperatures at a brisk 52 degrees. In a city where the litany of defeats takes on larger-than-life scale—The Drive, The Fumble, The Shot— Jackson decided to steer into the skid. He and others who went into the lake that day at Huntington Beach in Bay Village wore T-shirts calling the dip "The Cleanse." Proceeds from the event went to Jackson's charitable foundation, dedicated to combating human trafficking.

Jackson felt like he had been rinsed clean by healing waters.

"We're gonna cleanse ourselves, and we're going to be done with the past," he said in a video shared by the Browns. "Everything that's gone on in the past in the year 2016 and the year 2017, we're closing the book on. I truly believe that as we move forward that we're heading in the direction where we have a chance to win and win consistently."

Consistent winning has eluded the team since, but things are nowhere near as bad as they were when Jackson was the head coach. And whatever good fortune awaits the Browns, Jackson will only watch. He was fired as head coach halfway through the 2018 season.

ADVENTURES IN SPORTS OWNERSHIP

The history of sports is littered with interesting characters, from Rube Waddell, a pitcher who would stop games to watch airplanes fly overhead (in his defense, they were still a novelty at the time) to gunslinging quarterbacks like Ken Stabler, who said, "There's nothing wrong with studying the game plan by the light of the jukebox."

Personality doesn't end at the playing field's edges. It can be found in dugouts and sidelines—and even in the owner's box. The men who signed the checks for Cleveland sports teams ran the gamut, from Bill Veeck, whose irrepressible personality masked a brilliant baseball and business acumen; to Mickey McBride, the Browns' first owner, content to let Paul Brown work his magic; to Nick Mileti, the impresario who brought the NBA to Cleveland and owned pieces of several major league teams in Cleveland in the 1970s—even if his fortune was merely on paper.

Sometimes, though, the magnates who owned Cleveland's teams were a lot less beloved, from those who cast a wandering eye from the city's shoreline to those who proved that wealth didn't necessarily bring with it intelligence. Like they say at the beginning of *Law & Order*, these are their stories.

ROBBING CLEVELAND TO PAY ST. LOUIS—
THE SAD END OF THE CLEVELAND SPIDERS

Before the Indians, er, Guardians, there were the Cleveland Spiders. The Spiders began in the American Association before moving to the National League in 1889. Two years later, they built a new stadium at the corner of East 66th Street and Lexington Avenue near (not coincidentally) a stop for a streetcar line owned by Frank Robison, who also owned the Spiders. Their pitcher for the opener was a Tuscarawas County native named Denton Young, who'd acquired the nickname Cy, because he threw so hard that when he hit a fence with a pitched ball, it looked like a cyclone had struck.

The Spiders were regular contenders for the league title, in fact winning the Temple Cup, the prize for the end-of-year playoff between the first- and second-place teams, in 1895. But attendance was poor—due in part to blue laws that prohibited baseball on Sunday, at that time the only day when fans typically didn't work. Following the 1898 season, Robison bought, at a sheriff's sale, the Brown Stockings, a National League team in St. Louis that had declared bankruptcy. At the time, there was no rule prohibiting ownership of more than one team.

Robison then started transferring to his new team in St. Louis (renamed the Perfectos) any Cleveland player worth taking. The players left behind in Cleveland were called "the Misfits," and they set a record for futility unmatched since. The 1899 Spiders went 20-134 for a .129 winning percentage. (By comparison, the 1962 expansion Mets, who hold the modern record for losses in a season, went 40-120 for a winning percentage of .250.)

Their 134 losses included a staggering 101 road losses. Teams had no interest in coming to Cleveland to play the Spiders, since ticket sales wouldn't be enough to cover their travel expenses. Following the 1899 season, the National League dropped four teams. That the Spiders would be included was a foregone conclusion.

Cleveland would not be without a baseball team for long, though. An enterprising former sportswriter named Byron Bancroft "Ban" Johnson saw to that. Johnson was president of the Western League. In 1900, he shifted a team in that minor league from Columbus to Cleveland and the American League began. Next year, it declared itself a major league, and there's been a team in Cleveland ever since—known variously as the Blues, Bronchos and Naps before acquiring the nickname Indians starting in 1915 and eventually being renamed the Guardians after the 2021 season.

THE RAMS WIN—THEN LEAVE

The Cleveland Rams put together a season for the ages in 1945.

A doormat of the NFL since entering the league in 1937, the Rams played second fiddle to the league's powers, the Bears and the Packers. They'd even suspended operations in 1943 due to World War II. But in 1944, the Rams drafted Southern California native Bob Waterfield, nearly as famous for his pinup wife Jane Russell (they were high school sweethearts in Van Nuys) as he was for his talent as quarterback at UCLA.

Waterfield, under the tutelage of coach Adam Walsh and his brother, general manager Chile Walsh, piled up gaudy (for the era) numbers as a rookie quarterback, winning the NFL MVP award and leading the Rams to the NFL Championship Game. For the title game, the Rams eschewed the cozy confines of League Park— their home that season—to play before what they hoped to be a large home crowd at Cleveland Stadium. (At the time, the championship game alternated sites between the league's Western and Eastern Division champions.) On a frigid December day, the Rams beat the Washington Redskins 15-14. Waterfield threw two touchdown passes, and the only other Rams score came when Washington quarterback Sammy Baugh's pass out of his own end zone hit the goalpost and fell back into the end zone. Under the rules of the game at the time—changed the following year due to protests from team owner George Preston Marshall—it was a safety.

Great things appeared to be at hand for the Rams, a skilled team owned by a young, charismatic, visionary owner, Dan Reeves. And they were—just not in Cleveland. A month after the Rams won the championship, NFL owners approved Reeves' request to move the team to Los Angeles.

This was more than a decade before the Dodgers and Giants left New York for L.A. and San Francisco; the Rams were the first major league team to establish roots on the West Coast. Reeves said he was inspired to do so after watching college games and seeing the area's untapped potential for football fans.

Of course, at the same time plans were also being made for another pro football team, this one backed by Cleveland taxi magnate Mickey McBride and coached by and named for Northeast Ohio legend Paul Brown in Cleveland, and at best, the two teams would have shared an uneasy truce in the city. The Browns would be part of a new league that was also establishing a presence on the west coast, with teams in Los Angeles and San Francisco, inadvertently strengthening Reeves' case for the Rams to move, to head off any rivals.

The Rams would go on to win NFL championships in Los Angeles—and then a Super Bowl in St. Louis, where the team moved after the 1994 season, before returning to Southern California two decades later and winning a Super Bowl in 2022. They're the only team to win NFL championships in three different cities. And they're the only team to win a championship in one city and play in a different one the following year. Only in Cleveland.

GEORGE STEINBRENNER AND
THE CLEVELAND PIPERS

For decades, winter in Cleveland belonged to the Barons, an American Hockey League team billed as the seventh-best pro hockey team in the world, behind only the "Original Six" of the NHL. But the city's sports landscape was dotted with efforts at professional basketball.

In the 1920s, Max Rosenblum, owner of a clothing store in the city, sponsored an eponymous basketball team, first playing exhibitions and then as a founding member and three-time champion of the American Basketball League. That team folded in 1930. In 1946, Al Sutphin, the owner of the Barons, started a basketball team, the Rebels, in the Basketball Association of America, a forerunner of the NBA. The team lasted for just one year, folding due to lack of interest from the press and the public.

And in the 1950s, the Cleveland Pipers played in the National Industrial Basketball League. (The pro game has its roots in industrial leagues with semi-professional players. The Detroit Pistons are so called not because of any connection to the city's auto industry, but because they were sponsored by a piston company in their initial home, Fort Wayne, Indiana.) The Pipers were coached by John McLendon, a protégé of the game's inventor, James Naismith. In 1960, the team was sponsored by Kinsman Marine Transit, a well-established shipping company in Cleveland.

Around the same time, Abe Saperstein, the founder and promoter of the Harlem Globetrotters, then the most famous pro basketball team in the United States, was looking to form a pro league to rival the NBA. And the young treasurer for Kinsman, the son of the company's president and an athlete in his own right, was more than interested.

George Steinbrenner had competed in sports throughout his high school and collegiate career. He got a master's degree in physical education from Ohio State and had embarked on a football coaching career, with stops at Northwestern and Purdue, before being ordered home by his father to take his place in the family business. But his interest in sports had never waned.

The Pipers joined Saperstein's ABL in 1961 and won the championship that season under Steinbrenner's ownership. But as owner of the Pipers, Steinbrenner would demonstrate the same temperament and flaws that would manifest themselves over and over again through the ensuing decades after he bought the New York Yankees. The Pipers were nearly kicked out of the league. Players revolted as paychecks bounced (Steinbrenner had limited access to the family fortune). McLendon was fired. "He was not anti-black," McLendon later said, when asked if Steinbrenner was a racist, according to Bill Livingston's book *George Steinbrenner's Pipe Dream*. "He was anti-human. He treated everyone the same— like dogs."

Steinbrenner remained an unabashed fan of his alma mater, then one of the most successful college basketball teams in the country. He lured former Buckeye Larry Siegfried to Cleveland and tried to do the same with a pair of Ohio natives who had seen success with the Buckeyes: John Havlicek and Jerry Lucas.

Lucas was LeBron before LeBron, a celebrated high school athlete who'd won two state titles with Middletown before heading on to Ohio State, where he won a national title and twice was named the Final Four Most Outstanding Player. He also won a gold medal with the U.S. team at the 1960 Olympics. He was to that point the most accomplished amateur basketball player in the world. And Steinbrenner ended up signing him to a contract for the Pipers.

The move gave the team—if not the league—instant credibility. All of a sudden, Steinbrenner and the Pipers were being courted by the NBA, which already had a team in Ohio, the Cincinnati Royals (they would eventually become the Sacramento Kings). The NBA at the time was a regional league, offering territorial draft picks for teams to grab local talent. That's how Wilt Chamberlain, a Philadelphia native, ended up with the Warriors (initially a Philadelphia team before moving west) and Oscar Robertson, who'd played college basketball at the University of Cincinnati, ended up with the Royals. Now, the Royals felt like their territory was being invaded by Steinbrenner and the Pipers.

For the Pipers to join the NBA, it would cost $250,000—a relative pittance now, but a huge sum at the time. It was also money that George Steinbrenner didn't have—and his father wouldn't give him. The deal to join the NBA fell through, starting a chain reaction of unfortunate events. The Pipers ended up folding, which weakened the league so much that it, too, folded. Lucas ended up with the Royals. Steinbrenner and his investors ended up soaked. It was believed that Steinbrenner's abject failure had poisoned the well, and that no NBA team would ever come to Cleveland.

Steinbrenner did eventually buy into the NBA, becoming a minority owner of the Chicago Bulls when Bill Wirtz bought the team in 1972—a year before Steinbrenner bought the New York Yankees from CBS. In many ways, the NBA was still a fly-by-night organization, and the Bulls were mediocre—and poorly-capitalized. Tired of having to write checks with nothing to show for it, Steinbrenner cashed out when Wirtz sold the team to Jerry Reinsdorf. The deal was confirmed with a handshake before the 1984–85 season started. That fall, the Bulls took the court for the first time with their newest player, a rookie from North Carolina named Michael Jordan.

JIM BROWN'S FORCED RETIREMENT

Soon after Art Modell purchased the Browns in 1961, it was abundantly clear a new sheriff was in town.

Modell, a young advertising executive from New York, was a breed apart from the old guard of NFL owners like the Mara family in New York, Art Rooney in Pittsburgh and Papa Bear George Halas in Chicago. Modell had drinks with his players. He held court with reporters. And unlike his predecessors, as Browns owner, he was not content to sit back, sign the checks and let Paul Brown run the team.

Brown had always operated like a college or high school coach. That type of autocratic leadership worked with the returning World War II veterans on the Browns' first teams, but a new generation had supplanted them, including African American players, who chafed under Brown's heavy-handed paternalism—and were more than willing to tell Modell as much.

Among those players was Jim Brown, who threatened to quit the game rather than stay under Paul Brown's thumb. So in 1963, during a newspaper strike, Modell fired Paul Brown in a move that was likened to toppling the Terminal Tower. Blanton Collier succeeded his former mentor as head coach, and the Browns, behind the punishing running of Jim Brown, continued to contend.

The Browns beat the vaunted Baltimore Colts for the 1964 NFL title, and the next season lost the NFL Championship Game to Green Bay. After an ebb in the late 1950s, the Browns appeared on their way to another dynasty.

But on July 14, 1966, the Browns' aspirations took a body blow.

Jim Brown, in England filming *The Dirty Dozen*, announced he was retiring from the NFL. Just 30, he had already cemented himself as the greatest running back to that point. He'd played nine seasons, leading the league in rushing in eight of them, and was named the NFL MVP three times, including the previous season.

Filming on the movie, his second acting role, had run long—to the point where Modell issued an ultimatum to Brown: Show up for training camp starting July 17 at Hiram College or face a $100 daily fine. Brown didn't have a lot of leverage in that situation. All he could do . . . was walk away. "You can't fine me if I don't show up," he recalled in a 2015 *Sports Illustrated* interview.

At the peak of his NFL career, Jim Brown retired, devoting his life to acting and activism. The Browns failed to qualify for the playoffs in 1966, won the division in 1967 but lost in the playoffs to Dallas, and lost the NFL Championship Game the following two years—the last two NFL Championship Games before the AFL-NFL merger was formalized. Would Brown, who easily could have played another four years, have made the difference?

Paul Wiggin would know. He played 11 years for the Browns,

many of them as Brown's teammate. In 2015, he told *Sports Illustrated*, "I was a player for my time. Jim Brown was a player for all times." And Art Modell ran him off.

VERNON STOUFFER'S SALE OF THE INDIANS

A month after Jim Brown's retirement, the Indians franchise changed hands. The new owner was Vernon Stouffer, who had made his fortune first with his family's restaurants and then by branching out into ready-made frozen food. Stouffer's merged with Litton Industries, a company that made microwaves, in what seemed to be a natural partnership. Well capitalized and relying on a smart staff, it looked like things could be looking up for the Indians, who had spent the better part of the previous decade spinning their wheels. Indeed, for a time, the Indians were linked to any city in the late 1950s and early 1960s in search of a baseball team, including Houston, Minneapolis, Seattle and Oakland.

But much of Stouffer's wealth was tied up in stock, and when his investments took a tumble, so did his fortune. And while other cities got shiny new multipurpose stadiums, the Indians continued to play in front of oceans of empty seats at Cleveland Stadium, 40 years old and starting to look it. Other cities made entreaties to Stouffer, who'd turned down offers from ownership groups in Dallas and Washington. But his financial problems couldn't let him hold out forever. In 1971, the Indians started working on an agreement to play a slate of "home" games at the new domed stadium under construction in New Orleans.

At the same time, interested local buyers started inquiring about the Indians. Among them was a group of investors headed by former Tribe slugger Al Rosen, a link to the team's glory days in the early 1950s. Rosen's investors included George Steinbrenner, who even after his fiasco with the Pipers remained interested in buying a major league team—and was in a much better position to do so than he was a decade earlier.

Steinbrenner had bought out his father at Kinsman Marine Transit, and the company had switched from shipping ore to grain, which proved more lucrative in the 1960s. Kinsman also bought the American Shipping Company. Steinbrenner lobbied hard for passage of the Maritime Act of 1970, and with the tax breaks, incentives and contracts available, had made AmShip into a large and prosperous company.

In October 1971, it appeared a deal was at hand. Steinbrenner had leaked to the press that a sale was going to happen, with a final price around $9 million. But the deal was scuttled when an irate and likely inebriated Stouffer killed it, yelling that Rosen and Steinbrenner were trying to steal the team from him. (The bid from Washington was $10 million, and the Dallas deal he'd turned down was $15 million.)

Steinbrenner continued to look for a team to buy, and found one about a year later when he heard that CBS was ready and willing to unload the Yankees. By the time Steinbrenner bought the Yankees in January 1973—and promised to be a hands-off owner—Stouffer had sold the Tribe. The deal with Nick Mileti had been finalized in March 1972 for $10 million. Mileti, a lawyer, had succeeded twice where Steinbrenner had failed: He'd brought the NBA to Cleveland with the expansion Cavaliers, and now he'd bought the Indians. Steinbrenner, though, had the last laugh. He owned the Yankees until his death in 2010, a tempestuous relationship that included a suspension and a "lifetime" ban from Major League Baseball—and seven World Series wins.

Mileti was out of pro sports ownership by the end of the 1970s. Ostensibly, he was going into producing movies, but all of his sports purchases had been with other people's money, and he could only make it work for so long.

"When Stouffer sold it to Nick Mileti, instead of taking cash from George, he got Green Stamps," Indians President Gabe Paul is quoted as saying in Peter Golenbock's book *Wild, High and Tight*, a biography of Billy Martin that detailed Steinbrenner's ownership of the Yankees. "He didn't get paid off for a long time."

CLEVELAND'S TWO SEASONS
AS AN NHL CITY

Nick Mileti's foray into Cleveland sports began when he organized and promoted a game at the old Cleveland Arena between Niagara University and his alma mater, Bowling Green State University. The game turned out to draw a significant crowd, leading Mileti to believe that despite George Steinbrenner's ineptitude with the Pipers and Al Sutphin's indifference with the Rebels, there was a market for pro basketball in Cleveland.

Mileti paid the franchise fee for what turned out to be the Cavaliers and, to ensure there was a place for them to play, bought the Cleveland Arena. (One of the problems the Pipers had faced was no steady home court. They played home games at Public Hall downtown, the Arena, Baldwin-Wallace College, the Columbus Fairgrounds and Admiral King High School in Lorain!) Mileti knew the Arena was under-used. He recalled in a 2015 interview for *Ohio Magazine* that when he promoted the BG game, he looked at the calendar of events and saw, "It was all white. There were no events." The Arena also had a symbiotic relationship with Barons, the city's AHL team, and Mileti ended up buying them both.

The Arena had been built in the 1930s to try to lure an NHL team—likely the Montreal Canadiens, who were faltering amid ownership problems, money problems during the Depression and sharing the city with a Stanley Cup champion, the Maroons. But the Habs righted the ship, and Cleveland would have to wait to be an NHL city—40 more years, in fact.

There were efforts to join the NHL virtually every decade from then on. In 1972, Mileti bought a team in the new World Hockey Association, the Crusaders. The Barons were exiled to Florida and then folded. And in 1976, another NHL team, looking to stay afloat, made the move to Cleveland.

The NHL had expanded in 1967, doubling its size, including two teams on the West Coast, the Kings in Los Angeles and the Seals in the Bay Area. The Seals were known variously as the Oakland Seals, the California Seals and the California Golden Seals. (Owner Charlie Finley made sure the team had the same green, gold and white colors of his baseball team, the Oakland Athletics.). By the mid-1970s, the team was hemorrhaging money, particularly after a deal for a proposed San Francisco arena fell through. Minority stockholders George and Gordon Gund, Cleveland natives whose father ran the Cleveland Trust Co., said Cleveland would be the perfect landing spot, citing the city's slavish following of the departed Barons.

In Cleveland, the team was renamed the Barons—Mileti happily signed away the name, which he still owned, to the team's owners after they picked up the check for dinner—and began play in the fall of 1976 in the new "Palace on the Prairie," the Richfield Coliseum.

The Coliseum, which had opened two years earlier with a performance by Frank Sinatra, was a state-of-the-art facility and a marked improvement over the Arena. It was also in the middle of nowhere. Mileti thought suburban sprawl would get to Richfield, near the border between Summit and Cuyahoga counties, and he felt its location, not far from the Ohio Turnpike and Interstate 77, would allow the Cavs to draw regionally, throughout Ohio and into Pennsylvania and West Virginia.

But the Richfield location was discouraging for potential walk-up ticket sales, and the move came so quickly that the team couldn't sell a lot of season tickets. As a result, the Barons played to crowds even smaller than the ones they'd seen in the Bay Area as the Seals. And while Northern California weather could be a crapshoot, players would rather play there—where they could golf on days off—than in Cleveland, coincidentally during two of the worst winters in local and national history.

In fact, in early 1977, it looked like the team would be unable to make payroll, which was actually good news to players. Mike Fidler, a rookie that year, said if that was the case, they would have all become free agents and left the team as fast as they could. But a sudden infusion of cash kept the team afloat at least through the remainder of the season. The 1978 season was no better. There was no existential threat to the team, but there was another blizzard over the winter, tamping down attendance, and a 15-game winless streak.

Finally, at the NHL owners' meetings that summer, the plug was pulled. The Barons would merge with the Minnesota North Stars, and a dispersal draft would be held. Cleveland's brief time as a city with teams in all four major leagues had come to an ignominious close after just two years. It remains the last time a team in any of the four major sports has folded.

TED STEPIEN, "THE DUMBEST MAN IN PRO SPORTS"

On Jan. 20, 1983, Ted Stepien was having a busy day. Less than three years into his tenure as Cavaliers owner, he was looking for a way out. Stepien, a minority shareholder in the Indians (who were perpetually on the prowl for stockholders to provide capital in the 1970s), had bought the Cavs in 1980, becoming the team's fourth owner in as many months. The Cavs were in bad shape, a middling team that, like the Indians, were struggling to stay afloat.

Stepien, by comparison, was an all-American success story. A self-described "Polack from Pittsburgh," he had seen combat as part of a bomber crew in Europe and Africa during World War II, then returned to Cleveland, where he'd had his military training, and used his GI Bill benefits to attend Western Reserve University. He turned a $500 loan from his father into a multimillion-dollar firm, Nationwide Advertising, with offices throughout North America. He also owned a chain of Cleveland-area restaurants called the Competitors Club.

Like George Steinbrenner, Stepien had a sports itch he couldn't fully scratch. He had been an all-city football and basketball player

at Schenley High School and had turned down a football schol-
arship to Cornell University to join the Army Air Forces. But with
the Cavs, Stepien's sports management approach could charitably
be described as scorched earth. Immediately after taking over the
team, Stepien fired head coach Stan Albeck and replaced him with
Bill Musselman, a Wooster native, a Wittenberg graduate and a
former coach at Ashland University. Musselman was probably best
known in Ohio, though, as the Minnesota coach when the Gophers
brawled with the Buckeyes at the end of a game. A new Cavs song—a
polka, honoring Stepien's Polish roots—was unveiled, and a dance
team, the Teddi Bears, could soon be found on the Coliseum hard-
wood. Play-by-play man Joe Tait, who had been part of the Cavs
almost since the team started a decade earlier, went into exile for
being too critical of the Cavs on broadcasts. Stepien changed the
team's radio home in a fit of pique.

Stepien also had a quick trigger finger when it came to personnel moves. In the span of one calendar year, 1981, the Cavs had
FOUR different coaches—including one future Hall of Famer, who
was also fired quickly (but we'll get to that later) and Don Delaney,
a high school and college coach who'd coached Stepien's softball
team, the Competitors. When Stepien took a controlling interest
in the Cavs, he hired Delaney there—as general manager, a position he was inexperienced in and ill-prepared for. (Legend has it
when Stepien made the offer, Delaney said, "You want me to do
WHAT?")

Shortly after taking over ownership, Stepien traded star players
Campy Russell and Foots Walker. Then he started dealing draft
picks, not just for players, but for ineffectual players. Dallas Mavericks coach Dick Motta, a frequent trade partner at the time, said he
was afraid to go to lunch for fear he'd miss a call from Cleveland.
Ultimately, NBA Commissioner Larry O'Brien had to step in and
personally approve any trade the Cavs made.

"He is the person whom NBA owners use to scare their children
into staying in bed at night," sportswriter Charles P. Pierce wrote
decades later in Grantland. "Go to sleep, or Ted Stepien will trade

you to Milwaukee for a pound of Usinger's sausage and half a case of Blatz."

The Cavs kept losing, enough so that they were referred to as the "Cadavers." And Stepien kept losing money. The Coliseum was more like a mausoleum, and Stepien started looking to other cities—including Toronto. On Jan. 20, 1983, he met there with a potential buyer for the Cavs, and that evening, he made an appearance on a Toronto radio show, talking about selling to Canadian investors. As later recounted in the book *Cavs from Fitch to Fratello* by Joe Menzer and Burt Graeff, the show's host, Mark Hebschner, took a call from a listener: "Am I talking to the dumbest man in professional sports?" The caller sounded like a kid, but in actuality, it was Pete Franklin, host of the *Sportsline* radio show, which he boasted was heard in "38 states and half of Canada." Stepien had been one of Franklin's regular foils, at one point suing for $15 million, alleging slander by the radio host. (The suit was ultimately dropped.) Franklin dropped his fake voice and then, still on-air, proceeded to blast Stepien, calling him two-faced and a dumbbell.

Stepien ended up selling the team to local buyers, the Gund brothers, who would be far more successful in their efforts at pro basketball in Cleveland than they were in their efforts at pro hockey in Cleveland. But first, they had to buy several draft picks because Stepien had traded away the Cavs' picks for years to come. To this day, it's against NBA rules for a team to trade away first-round picks in back-to-back years.

It's known as the Stepien rule.

THE DONALD AND THE TRIBE

Before he was president, before he was host of *The Apprentice*, before even his first best-seller, *The Art of the Deal*, Donald Trump was a man who was looking to buy a Major League Baseball team.

Trump's father had made his family's fortune in real estate development in New York's outer boroughs. But Trump wanted to make a splash in Manhattan, nationally and internationally. Tony Grossi, then of the *Plain Dealer*, wrote at the time that Trump seemed like "a man who awakes in a cold sweat with the frightening realization that a billion Chinese never heard of him."

And Trump wanted to own a sports team. He'd kicked the tires on his hometown Mets as well as the Giants. He'd made an offer to buy the Minnesota Twins, but owner Calvin Griffith instead sold to Carl Pohlad—at a lower price than Trump's offer.

In 1983, the same year Stepien was shopping around for a new owner for the Cavs, Donald Trump's attorney initially sent a letter that February to the Indians professing the magnate's interest in buying the team, owned since 1978 by Steve O'Neill. Trump had also talked with team president Gabe Paul about buying the Indians. After O'Neill died that August, his estate was considering all potential buyers, and Trump made a bid once again, for $34 million— far more than any other offer being made at that point. However, there were two big potential dealbreakers: Trump owned casino interests, a strict no-no for any MLB owner, and he offered no long-term commitment to staying in Cleveland. He was willing to sign a short-term lease, but he knew the key to success for the Indians would be a new stadium—in Cleveland or somewhere else.

Ultimately, the deal fell through, and that September, Trump bought a team in the United States Football League, the New Jersey Generals.

Trump occupied himself with his USFL team—right up until he led the league into direct competition with the NFL and ensuing ruin. Trump at least talked about buying the Mets in the early 2010s, and tried to buy the Buffalo Bills after owner Ralph Wilson died.

In the end, it would be another three years before O'Neill's estate sold the Indians—to different real estate developers, brothers David and Richard Jacobs. And they would succeed in getting the new stadium.

ART MODELL'S PURSUIT OF ANDRE RISON

Bill Belichick's first three years as Browns coach definitely showed an upward trend after the team had bottomed out under Bud Carson, but it wasn't until year four that things finally came together. In 1994, the Browns went 11-5, their first winning record in five years, then the longest such drought in the team's history. (Ahhh, those were the days . . .). They advanced to the playoffs and beat the Patriots in a wild card game before losing to the Steelers in the divisional round.

The Browns needed a splashy move that would put them over the top—and that move, owner Art Modell decided, would be signing talented free-agent wide receiver Andre Rison. In a bit of ominous foreshadowing, the deal was an open secret well before it was formally announced. The five-year, $17 million deal—chump change now—made Rison the highest-paid wide receiver in the NFL.

"He's the biggest star we've signed," Modell told the *Plain Dealer* at the time. "He is truly a potential Hall of Famer."

Rison, for his part, was excited to be in Cleveland. He'd grown up a Browns fan in Michigan, and was looking for a chance to win a Super Bowl—which he thought the Browns had. He was hardly alone. Even *Sports Illustrated* thought the Browns could go to the Super Bowl that year.

Rison's only guaranteed money was a $5 million signing bonus, and Modell said his own financial situation was so precarious that he had to go to five different banks to get a loan to pay for it, not reassuring words from a man who was supposed to be independently wealthy. Modell later claimed, when he announced in November 1995 the team would be moving to Baltimore, that he had been hemorrhaging money for years.

Partway through the 1995 season, the Browns were 4-5, still within reach of a playoff spot, when the bottom then fell out, and the team won just one more game that year—its finale at Cleveland Stadium, against the Bengals.

Modell was hiding out, trying to finish the deal to take the Browns to Baltimore, but Rison could be seen every Sunday and rightly or wrongly, he bore the brunt of the abuse from fans upset about the impending move and the lack of production from Rison, who was a bad fit in the offense in his lone year in Cleveland. He joked that by the end of the season, his nickname was "Boo."

As it turns out, Rison wouldn't spend any time in Baltimore, either. The team cut him that offseason. Ultimately, he got his Super Bowl ring following the 1996 season—with the Packers, against the Patriots. Bill Belichick, Rison's coach in Cleveland, watched from the opposing sideline as a Patriots assistant. He'd also been unceremoniously dumped after the team's move to Baltimore.

Rison was denied another chance at a Super Bowl four years later with the Raiders, when they lost to the Ravens in the AFC Championship Game. The Ravens were on the way to Art Modell's only Super Bowl win. And counter to Modell's prediction, Canton has not come calling for Andre Rison.

THE CAVS GET "BAMBOOZERED"

In 2002, the Cavaliers struck gold in the NBA Draft. Duke University's Carlos Boozer fell to the second round, and the Cavs picked him up with the 35th overall pick. As a rookie, Boozer averaged 10 points and 7.5 rebounds a game. The Cavs still finished tied with the Nuggets for the worst overall record in the NBA. However, that turned out to be fortuitous, as the Cavs got the top overall draft pick in that year's lottery, which they used to draft a recent high school graduate from just down the road in Akron. Perhaps you've heard of him . . . LeBron James?

Throughout his high school career at Akron St. Vincent-St. Mary, James had been the next big thing. Some of his games were nationally televised. He'd been on the cover of *Sports Illustrated* and coverage of him dominated the pages of his hometown newspaper, the *Akron Beacon Journal*. But the players he was joining were entirely unimpressed—including Boozer, who said in an interview on Akron's WVPX-TV, "We have better players than him at his position already on our team though." (To his credit, Boozer did recognize James' potential, saying, "The sky's the limit.")

James and Boozer clicked immediately. James demonstrated that his reputation wasn't entirely hype, and Boozer continued to be a strong scorer and rebounder for the Cavs, who had an 18-win improvement but fell short of the playoffs that season. Boozer had one more year left on his rookie contract, an option year for which he'd get paid $695,000. Negotiations were ongoing between Boozer, his agent at SFX and Cavs management, all of whom recognized that Boozer was outperforming his rookie contract. The Cavs also wanted to keep him long term but were hamstrung by salary cap issues.

As later reported by the Associated Press and *Sports Illustrated*, Cavs general manager Jim Paxson made a "handshake deal" with Boozer under which the team would decline his option, then Boozer would re-sign a six-year, $41 million contract, the most the Cavs could offer at that point. (If the Cavs instead picked up Boozer's option, they could have matched any offer made to him the following year as a free agent.)

At least Paxson and team owner Gordon Gund thought this deal was in place.

But when Boozer's option was declined, Boozer turned around and signed a six-year, $68 million deal with the Utah Jazz, which the Cavs would be unable to match.

It had been less than a decade since Art Modell moved the Browns, and Cleveland fans were feeling betrayed all over again. A new word entered the lexicon: Bamboozered. As in, Gordon Gund and the Cavs got Bamboozered.

Gund issued a public letter, a then-rare step from a Cavaliers owner. In it, he detailed what had happened, first issuing a *mea culpa* and saying that Paxson didn't deserve the blame he was getting, adding, "Any criticism should be directed to me, not to Jim Paxson. I want to be very clear that any fault is mine."

Gund said repeated discussions over the previous year had led him to believe that Boozer, out of a desire to stay in Cleveland and provide for his own financial security, would re-sign with the Cavs immediately if the option was declined. Boozer later said he could not have made any type of commitment like that, noting it was against the rules of the current NBA collective bargaining agreement. But it didn't matter. He'd been painted as the villain, a player who'd swindled a blind man.

"In the final analysis, I decided to trust Carlos and show him the respect he asked for," Gund wrote. "He did not show that trust and respect in return."

Boozer wasn't the only one who caught flack for the move. SFX ended up not just cutting ties with the player, but with the agent that had represented him in the deal, Rob Pelinka. (He's gone on to do all right for himself; he got to hoist a championship trophy in 2020 as general manager of the Lakers.)

In the popular "What If" parlor game of Cleveland sports—What if Jim Brown didn't retire when he did? What if George Steinbrenner bought the Indians?—Boozer's absence from Cleveland remains a second-tier question, particularly since eventually, James and the Cavaliers did win a title. But it's tantalizing to think what a young James, who dragged a grossly undermanned Cavs team to the 2007 NBA Finals, could have done with Boozer at his side.

DAN GILBERT'S LETTER

There's an old saw that history repeats itself first as tragedy and then as farce. Almost six years to the day after Gordon Gund wrote his letter to fans about the Carlos Boozer episode, his successor as Cavs owner, Dan Gilbert, wrote another. It was not as dignified.

Once again, it was about a player's departure. LeBron James had announced on prime-time television on July 8, 2010, that he'd be taking his talents to South Beach, joining the Miami Heat. Unlike Boozer, James really was a free agent. He was entirely within his rights to sign with whatever team he pleased, and in fact, would make less money with the Heat than he could have with a max deal with the Cavs.

Later that evening, Dan Gilbert published an open letter that was later described variously as insane, infamous and unhinged. Written in comic sans font, to the mystification of typesetting fans everywhere, the letter seethed with anger at James' "cowardly betrayal." It also included a promise that even at the time appeared motivated more by anger than reality: "I PERSONALLY GUARANTEE THAT THE CLEVELAND CAVALIERS WILL WIN AN NBA CHAMPIONSHIP BEFORE THE SELF-TITLED FORMER 'KING' WINS ONE." And yes, he wrote it in all caps.

The message tapped a vein with some irate Cavs fans, but to others, it was like the drunk uncle at a funeral screaming, "I NEVER LIKED YOU ANYWAY!"

LeBron's sojourn to Miami was successful. He played four years there, and the Heat advanced to the NBA Finals all four years, winning twice. Eventually, James and Gilbert had a heart-to-heart and mended fences. James said he regretted the ESPN special, and Gilbert said he regretted the letter, which remained on the Cavs website (although you did have to go looking for it) until 2014—shortly before James announced he was leaving Miami . . . to return to Cleveland.

This time, his announcement was far more subdued, with an article in *Sports Illustrated*.

In James' ensuing four years in Cleveland, the Cavs enjoyed a run of success unparalleled in their history, advancing to the Finals each year—each time meeting the Golden State Warriors—and winning one, coming back from a 3-1 series deficit to beat the vaunted Warriors, who had set an NBA record with 73 wins that season.

When that contract was up, James left again, this time for Los Angeles. That departure was even more low-key, with a Sunday night announcement via social media. Gilbert wrote another letter, this one far more magnanimous, closing with, "LeBron, you came home and delivered the ultimate goal. Nothing but appreciation and gratitude for everything you put into every moment you spent in a Cavaliers uniform. We look forward to the retirement of the famous #23 Cavs jersey one day down the line..."

THE FBI RAID ON PILOT FLYING J

On April 15, 2013, the world was rocked as a pair of improvised explosive devices made from pressure cookers blew up near the end of the route of the Boston Marathon, one of the most celebrated running races in America. The explosions killed three and injured hundreds, sparking a week-long manhunt for the suspects.

The news out of Boston completely overshadowed another story happening in Tennessee, as FBI and IRS agents served search warrants at the Knoxville headquarters of Pilot Flying J, the truck stop chain. Records were searched and confiscated, and subpoenas were served.

What did this have to do with Cleveland sports?

The chain of nearly 500 truck stops across the nation, one of the largest privately held companies in the United States, began with a single gas station in Tennessee, started by Jim Haslam in 1958. Haslam's younger son Bill had gone on to get elected mayor of Knoxville and then governor of Tennessee, and his older son Jimmy had owned the Cleveland Browns for less than a year when the offices were raided.

Haslam, like his father, had gone to the University of Tennessee and was a major booster, as well as a fan and friend of the school's most celebrated football alumnus, Peyton Manning. When the Steelers had to restructure, Haslam was taken on as a minority stockholder. And when Randy Lerner was looking to sell the Browns, Haslam was eager to buy the team. After the sale was finalized in October 2012, Haslam announced he was stepping down from Pilot Flying J to devote his time to owning the Browns. But the following February—two months before the investigation became public knowledge—Haslam announced his return, saying running the truck stops was his "first love."

At the root of the federal raid were allegations of widespread fraud in rebates to trucking lines. Meanwhile, the Browns went from bad to worse. As the Pilot Flying J case wound through court, a best-case scenario for Browns fans became the idea that maybe Haslam would be forced to sell the team.

All told, 14 former Pilot employees pleaded guilty, three more were convicted at trial and two more were given immunity in exchange for testimony. Haslam was never charged in relation to the investigation.

DRAFTING JOHNNY FOOTBALL

Chaos reigned following the 2013 Browns season. First, head coach Rob Chudzinski was fired after just one year at the helm. Then, after an exhaustive search—needed mostly because every attractive candidate wanted nothing to do with the trash fire the Browns had become—the Browns hired Mike Pettine as head coach. THEN Jimmy Haslam fired team CEO Joe Banner and General Manager Mike Lombardi, elevating assistant GM Ray Farmer to the top spot. It was Haslam's second housecleaning since taking over the team less than two years earlier.

At least the Browns held a multitude of picks in the 2014 draft, including two in the first round. After another miserable season, they would draft fourth. They also held the 26th pick in the first round, which they'd gotten from the Colts for Trent Richardson. The Browns ended up trading first-round picks with the Bills, who took wide receiver Sammy Watkins fourth overall. Now in the ninth spot, the Browns traded up one place with Minnesota to draft Justin Gilbert, a cornerback from Oklahoma State. In his own way, Gilbert was a spectacular failure. But he's not the Browns disaster fans remember from the first round.

As the evening wore on, a trade was announced. The Browns had dealt with the Eagles to move up again, from 26 to 22. It was a pick fraught with bad history for the Browns. Twice within the previous seven years, they'd drafted a quarterback there. Both—Brady Quinn and Brandon Weeden—had eminently forgettable playing careers. Yet once again, apparently thinking the third time was the charm, the Browns drafted a quarterback at number 22. This time, it was Johnny Manziel, the Texas A&M quarterback probably just as well-known for his off-field antics as his on-field improvisation.

What made Manziel the Browns' pick? His victory over Alabama? Becoming the first freshman to win the Heisman Trophy? His ability to run as well as throw? Well, as Manziel was being introduced as the draft pick, ESPN's Sal Paolantonio revealed that it was due to the influence of an unlikely source. Paolantonio related a conversation he had had with Browns owner Jimmy Haslam, and recalled Haslam saying, "I was out to dinner recently, and a homeless person was out on the street, looked up at me and said 'Draft Manziel.'"

The move instantly galvanized Browns fans, who rushed out to buy Manziel jerseys and jammed the phones to try to buy season tickets.

But otherwise it failed spectacularly. Manziel would be out of the league after just two years.

Illustrating the passion of the Browns fan base, Paolantonio noted that Haslam at that point could walk through Tennessee virtually unnoticed, but he was a celebrity in Cleveland. But the results of the Johnny Football Experiment led a lot of Browns fans to say, "Well, that's what you get for taking a homeless guy's advice."

FRONT OFFICE FOLLIES

"If they want you to cook the dinner, at least they ought to let you shop for some of the groceries." Bill Parcells said that in a news conference when leaving the Patriots. As head coach he had taken New England to a Super Bowl, and before that had won two Super Bowls with the Giants. Now, he wanted more than sideline duties; he wanted personnel duties, too.

Behind every successful team is some type of personnel authority. The job title has changed through the years. Sometimes they're team presidents, sometimes they're directors, but the most common term is general manager. (The first person to hold that title with a sports team? Hall of Fame umpire Billy Evans, who retired to become the Indians general manager in 1927.)

Whatever the title, though, when you're managing personnel, things don't always go smoothly. And in Cleveland, to follow with the Big Tuna's cooking metaphor, a lot of kitchen fires have been started.

TRADER LANE'S REIGN

To Indians fans of a certain age, Frank "Trader" Lane is excoriated as the man who traded Rocky Colavito, the slugging outfielder who was a fan favorite.

But that's not completely fair. Lane was known for plenty of boneheaded moves throughout Major League Baseball. But in spite of that, he managed to spend a lifetime in the game. There was always a team down on its luck that was willing to give him a shot.

Lane, a Cincinnati native, loved sports, even playing briefly for the Dayton Triangles football team (an early member of the NFL) and for a Class D team in Marion, Ohio owned by a local newspaper publisher who went on to be president, Warren Harding. But Lane just wasn't good at sports. So he started officiating, in baseball, football and basketball. While refereeing football games, he met Larry MacPhail, another referee, who was president of the Columbus Red Birds, a minor-league team that had become part of the Cardinals farm system. MacPhail moved on to become president of the Reds in 1933, and there he hired Lane, who within four years was running that team's farm system.

After the Japanese attack on Pearl Harbor plunged the United States into World War II, Lane joined the Navy—at 47! He kept in fighting trim throughout most of his adult life, and when he returned from his service (which saw him visiting bases in the Pacific, North Africa and Europe to build athletic facilities), he ended up back with MacPhail, who was by then with the Yankees.

In 1949, at the age of 53, Lane took his first job as a general manager, with the White Sox. It was regarded as a radioactive job; the team's ownership was a mess. Original owner Charles Comiskey had died in 1931, and the team passed to the hands of his son J. Louis Comiskey, who died himself eight years later. His widow Grace and her three children continued to own the team, and one of the reasons Lane was hired was to train Chuck Comiskey, Grace's only son and the heir apparent.

Lane's wheeling and dealing bore fruit. He traded for Minnie Minoso, the team's first Black player, as well as Nellie Fox, a future Hall of Famer. He also signed Luis Aparicio, another future Hall of Famer. Fox and Aparicio were a historic infield tandem that would help lead the White Sox to the 1959 pennant.

Lane also learned an important lesson: Trades kept his name in the papers, usually in 70-point headline type. He was so successful in Chicago, in fact, that when the moribund St. Louis Browns moved to Baltimore, they tried to lure him away to be their general manager. But the White Sox signed him to an extension, even though his relationship with Chuck Comiskey was starting to fray. Ultimately, Lane resigned, but Comiskey later said hiring him was the best move he'd ever made.

Lane's reputation at that point was stellar—and probably kept getting him jobs long after the Comiskeys sold the White Sox. His next stop was the St. Louis Cardinals. That team had been the class of the National League in the 1930s and 1940s, but had surrendered its pre-eminence to the Dodgers and, to a lesser extent, the Giants. Lane instantly set to work, putting everyone he could on the trading block, dealing Bill Virdon to Pittsburgh in what he later called the worst deal he ever made. Then Harvey Haddix went to Philadelphia, and Red Schoendienst, one of just two remaining players from the team's last World Series win in 1946, went to the Braves. The other player from those pennant-winning teams in the 1940s was, of course, Stan Musial. No less an authority than Commissioner Ford Frick called him baseball's perfect knight, and a statue of him stands in front of Busch Stadium.

Lane had to be talked out of trading Musial, too.

In 1957, Lane was named *The Sporting News* Executive of the Year, but he had worn out his welcome in St. Louis, and the owners were more than happy to let him resign. As luck would have it, the Indians had just fired Hank Greenberg as general manager (he remained a part owner of the team). Lane quickly signed on as Indians general manager. For most of the previous decade, the Tribe had been finishing second to the Yankees in the American League—except, of course, for 1948, when they won the World Series, and 1954, when they won 111 games to run away with the pennant. But they, like the Cardinals, were starting to slip.

Almost immediately, Lane started making moves. He fired manager Bobby Bragan (see "The Curse of Bobby Bragan" in

"Coaching Ain't Easy"), replacing him with former Indians infielder Joe Gordon, and dealt away Early Wynn, bringing Minnie Minoso back to Cleveland, where he'd started his career. At the trade deadline in June 1958, Lane made a deal with the Kansas City Athletics for Woodie Held and Vic Power, both of whom would go on to be regular contributors for the Indians. Among the pieces dealt to Kansas City was a crew-cut prospect from the tundra of North Dakota: Roger Maris, who, of course, ended up with the Yankees, winning two World Series and hitting 61 home runs during the 1961 season. He then won another World Series with the Cardinals.

In the short term, Lane's early moves for the Indians seemed to bear fruit. The team drew nearly 1.5 million fans in 1959, remaining in a tight pennant race with the White Sox. But he and Gordon clashed, and Gordon announced with less than two weeks left in the season he would resign. After the White Sox clinched the pennant—thanks in no small part to that year's Cy Young Award winner, Early Wynn—Lane fired Gordon. He then threw the sun, the moon and the stars at Leo Durocher in an effort to get him to manage the Indians, but came away empty-handed—and had to bring back Gordon.

Before the 1960 season, Lane traded Colavito to Detroit, for Harvey Kuenn. The move was so shocking that it was announced in downtown movie theaters as soon as word got out. Lane famously said that the deal was like trading hamburger for steak. And although the Indians got just one season out of Kuenn, Lane stood by the deal., "If I had it to do all over again, I'd still trade that Dago fruit peddler," he is quoted as saying in *The Cleveland Indians Encyclopedia* by Russell Schneider. Colavito, for his part, was just as diplomatic, telling his biographer, Mark Sommer, "Frank Lane was the biggest asshole who ever lived."

Five days before the Colavito trade, Lane made another deal that was nearly as damaging, trading away first baseman Norm Cash—whom he had first signed as an amateur free agent with the White Sox in 1955—to the Detroit Tigers for Steve Demeter. Cash had been acquired by the Indians in a five-player deal at the end of

1959 that sent Minnie Minoso to the White Sox for the second time. Cash went on to win a batting title in 1961 (an outlier year that may have been aided by doctored bats), and was the Tigers' everyday first baseman for the next decade. He remained a Detroit fan favorite until his premature death in 1986.

Lane wasn't done dealing with the Tigers. Halfway through the 1960 season, Lane decided he was fed up with Gordon, and engineered another trade, sending Gordon to Detroit, and getting Jimmie Dykes in return, who became the new Tribe manager.

Finally, after the 1960 season, the Indians were only too happy to let Frank Lane go. His final tally in Cleveland was 49 deals, involving 108 players, in a little over three seasons.

"I'm afraid to go to Cleveland," said Bob Hope, the comedian and Cleveland native who was a minority owner of the team. "Frank Lane might trade me."

Lane spent less than a year with the Athletics, clashing with owner Charlie Finley (who was described by legendary sportswriter Jim Murray as a self-made man who worshiped his creator). He then served as a scout for the Orioles, who were run by that time by Lee MacPhail, Larry's son. In the early 1970s, he so dazzled a young used-car dealer who was owner of the newest major league team in Milwaukee that the dealer, Bud Selig, hired Lane as general manager of the Brewers. He spent a year there as GM and was a scout afterward, later working for the Padres and the Texas Rangers. He died in Texas in 1981 at the age of 86.

"He went to sleep with his own convoluted reasoning and the waiver list underneath his pillow, and all he ever needed when in action was an ample supply of throat spray, a telephone, a pad and a book full of numbers," Hank Kram wrote for *Sports Illustrated* in 1968. "During his career he executed over 500 deals, some with craft, all with desperation." (Remember, this was prior to his time as Brewers general manager.) "The frequency of his trades, whether the result of some psychological compulsion or just an extension of his personality, was his strength and, at times, his weakness."

More often than not, his weakness. As the years went on and

the losses piled up for the Indians, writer Terry Pluto started to talk about the Curse of Rocky Colavito, how the trade so vexed the Tribe that they were doomed for a generation.

It might have been more appropriate to call it the curse of Trader Lane.

TRADED FOR HIMSELF

Harry Chiti's Major League Baseball career was relatively unspectacular—except for one brief moment in 1962. OK, two.

Chiti, a catcher, had bounced around the majors, with stints with the Cubs, the Athletics and the Tigers, as well as in the Yankees' and Orioles' minor league systems. It was the Orioles that traded him to Cleveland in November 1961. He was one of three players dealt for second baseman Johnny Temple. "I don't mind being traded," Temple said (according the book *Johnny Temple*, by William A. Cook). "But how could they trade me for Harry Chiti?"

Chiti, as it turned out, would never play a game for the Indians. 1962 marked the inaugural year of the National League's two new teams, the Houston Colt .45s (later Astros) and the New York Mets, whose hilarious ineptitude made them a fan favorite and inspired Casey Stengel to wail, "Can't anyone here play this game?" Writer Jimmy Breslin heard Stengel's plea and used it as a book title.

The Indians at that time weren't as inept as the expansion Mets, but they were no longer one of the stalwarts of the American League. Still, the Mets were happy to take Chiti for cash—Chiti said the money was used for a new scoreboard at Cleveland Stadium—and a player to be named later, a common term in baseball trans-actions.

Chiti played in 15 games for the Mets, his last coming on June 10, 1962, against the Cubs at Wrigley Field. He then was informed he'd been traded, and was ordered to report to Jacksonville to the Triple-A team there—which was an Indians affiliate.

The Mets must have saved the receipt. Harry Chiti was the player to be named later in his own trade.

Chiti spent the remainder of the 1962 season and parts of the following two seasons in the minor leagues before hanging it up. He then went to work as a deputy sheriff in Tennessee, where he would occasionally run into Cubs fans who remembered him from the 1950s—and people who remembered him as the answer to a trivia question, the player who had been traded for himself.

"And I sure do keep hearing about it," Chiti told the *South Florida Sun Sentinel* in 1986.

THE BEST TEAM BUBBLE-GUM CARDS COULD MAKE

In 1970, the city of Cleveland became home to an NBA team, the Cavaliers. They would play—at least initially—at the venerable Cleveland Arena on Euclid Avenue. Now all they needed was a team.

Owner Nick Mileti knew Bill Fitch, then the University of Minnesota head coach, from his days as the head coach at Mileti's alma mater, Bowling Green State University. Fitch was hired as the first Cavs coach, bringing along Jim Lessig, who'd been an assistant for him at Minnesota and Bowling Green (where he later served as athletic director). Now they just had to assemble some players.

With their familiarity with college basketball, Fitch and Lessig had a pretty good idea of the college players they wanted to take in the upcoming NBA Draft. But they were less familiar with current NBA talent who might be available in the expansion draft two months later. The expansion draft was needed because three new teams entered the league that year, the Cavs, the Portland Trail Blazers and the Buffalo Braves (now the Los Angeles Clippers). The sports landscape was markedly different in 1970, particularly in the NBA. Television coverage was largely regional—even the

NBA Finals were shown on tape-delay—and coaches would phone in game results to their hometown newspapers like they were high school teams!

"Back then, the only place to get the statistics and even a picture for a player was on a bubble gum card," Fitch recalled in a 2015 interview for *Ohio Magazine*. And that's exactly what he did. Lessig sent his son to area drug stores to buy the cards, and Lessig and Fitch used them to put together their version of a draft board.

The Cavs were miserable that first year, winning just 15 games, but they assembled a lineup of serviceable NBA players, and even got one of their future stalwarts, Bobby "Bingo" Smith, through the expansion draft. (Smith's number hangs in the rafters of Rocket Mortgage FieldHouse.)

"People made a lot of fun of us for it," Fitch said. "But [Knicks coach] Red Holzman said, 'By God, I'm going to do that!'"

PETER BAVASI'S "INDIAN UPRISING" IN CLEVELAND

When Peter Bavasi was named Indians President and Chief Operating Officer in 1984, the move was met with some concern.

Sure, he was to the manor born, having apprenticed with his father, legendary Dodgers GM Buzzie Bavasi, and was an experienced baseball man. But after leaving the Blue Jays in 1981—"They got sick of me, and I got sick of them," he told the *Plain Dealer* about the relationship, which ended with his resignation or firing, depending on who you asked—he had worked as a consultant with groups from Indianapolis and Tampa-St. Pete who were looking for a major league team. The Indians had been on the verge of moving for the better part of the last three decades. Was this finally how the team would abandon Cleveland?

Bavasi initiated a wholesale housecleaning. Gabe Paul, a baseball lifer who'd spent more than 20 years in total with the Indians (he went to New York to serve as part of Steinbrenner's management team when he bought the Yankees, but returned to Cleveland within a few years), was nudged into retirement, as was long-time team vice president Phil Seghi. Scouting director Bob Quinn was fired as well. Bavasi wanted his people in the front office. (Bob DiBiasio has been with the Indians since 1979, except for one year, 1987, which he spent in exile in Atlanta after being fired by Bavasi.)

Bavasi's changes weren't limited to the front office. On his watch, the Indians imposed new restrictions on what banners made by fans could say. Uniforms were changed, with no mention of the city of Cleveland on jerseys, and the caps were adorned only with Chief Wahoo; the C, which had adorned caps for as long as the team had been around, was removed. All this gave further fuel to rumors the team would leave. Complimentary ticket giveaways were severely curtailed. Even famed outfield drummer John Adams now had to pay his own way, prompting him to tell the *Los Angeles Times*, "I hope Bavasi buys a free agent with the $2 he gets from my tickets."

But at least in the short term, it seemed to work. Although the 1985 Indians bottomed out with 102 losses—tying a record for the worst record in team history—the following year the team won 84 games and prospects looked bright on the field.

They looked better off the field as well. Steve O'Neill's estate had finally found a buyer committed to keeping the team in Cleveland, brothers Richard and David Jacobs, Akron natives who had made their fortune in real estate development.

New ownership invariably meant new management, though, and Bavasi resigned in early 1987 to take over Telerate, a news service providing financial information in real time to investors. He has not worked for a major league team since.

"I've done my job here," Bavasi told the *Plain Dealer* when news broke of his resignation. "All the pieces are in place."

That turned out to be not even close to the truth. Although *Sports Illustrated* picked the Indians to win the World Series in 1987, in the now-notorious "Indian Uprising" cover, the team lost 101 games. It was the second of three times in a seven-year span that the team lost at least 100 games.

"GO ROOT FOR BUFFALO"

The Browns and Buffalo Bills have always had a strange relationship. Less than 200 miles apart, the two Lake Erie port cities are united by cold weather and pro football heartbreak. The Browns' losses in AFC championship games in the 1980s gave way to the Bills' four straight Super Bowl losses, a feat unmatched in pro sports. (And can we just stop for a minute and appreciate what an achievement making it to the Super Bowl FOUR YEARS IN A ROW is? I feel like the Bills don't get enough credit for that.)

Two teams voted against Art Modell's proposed move to Baltimore. One was the Steelers; the other was the Bills. In the three years Cleveland was without a team (or as I like to think of it, the three years the Browns were undefeated), the Bills would invite Browns fans to attend a game in Buffalo.

Throughout the 2000s, both teams had more failures than success, with the Bills at one point holding the longest playoff drought in the NFL and the Browns not that far behind. But in 2007, the Browns won 10 games (although they failed to make the playoffs), and coach Romeo Crennel and GM Phil Savage appeared to be the right personnel to lead the Browns, and both were given hefty extensions following the season.

Crennel was a longtime assistant to Bill Belichick and had been on the Browns sidelines with Chris Palmer before he was hired as head coach following Butch Davis' abrupt departure. And Savage was a wunderkind of the league. He'd served as a scout for Belichick with the Browns before rising to personnel director for the Ravens under Ozzie Newsome. He left Baltimore in 2005 to serve as Browns general manager.

But the Browns stumbled out of the gate in 2008, losing their first three games. The team's fortunes never really improved. Their success the season before appeared to be a mirage. There were bright spots, though. The team beat the Giants, who had won the Super Bowl the previous season, decisively on Monday night. After the team won a hard-fought victory over the Bills on Nov. 17, a story broke on the website Deadspin about a fan who had emailed Savage to voice his displeasure, writing, "You are easily the worst GM in the NFL. This is officially a regime that is worse than Butch Davis." The letter writer noted that he'd composed the email while the Browns were leading—a lead they'd kept, unlike the week before, when a 13-point lead evaporated in a loss to Denver.

Savage's reply was short and to the point. "Go root for Buffalo-f#@* you"

At first, the chain of custody with the email was called into question—not necessarily an unreasonable accusation. After all, who could believe that an NFL general manager would, first, respond to fans and, second, do so in such a manner?

But within a couple days, Savage acknowledged the correspondence. "It happened," he told the Associated Press. "We have both apologized to each other since."

As it turned out, that win over Buffalo was the Browns' last of the season. The team lost six straight afterward to end the season 4-12, and Crennel and Savage were both shown the door.

"DON'T COME TO ME FOR PLAYOFF TICKETS"

Browns head coach Eric Mangini's days were already numbered by the end of his first season as Browns coach in 2009.

That's when Browns owner Randy Lerner hired Mike Holmgren, at the time just four years removed from coaching the Seahawks to a Super Bowl appearance. Holmgren was regarded as an offensive guru, from his work as a 49ers assistant with Joe Montana and Steve Young to his time as Packers head coach, when he led Green

Bay to one Super Bowl win and another appearance, both with Brett Favre.

But Holmgren didn't come to Cleveland to coach. Lerner gave him the keys to the castle as team president. (Shortly before taking the role in Cleveland, he'd turned down an administrative position in Seattle because he wouldn't have enough power in the role.)

Holmgren had no plans to fire Eric Mangini, giving him another year as coach. But when Mangini went 5-11 in his second year, just like he did in his first year, he was fired.

Holmgren then hired Pat Shurmur, whose uncle Fritz had been Holmgren's defensive coordinator in Green Bay. It was a seamless transition, as Shurmur went 4-12 his first year as coach. But Holmgren said the team was on the right path.

"You can choose to believe me or you can say, 'I've heard it before,'" Holmgren said during a news conference that December. "That's your choice, but when it does happen, don't come to me for extra tickets to a playoff game or something. Don't do that.

"You're either with us or you're not. I'm telling you it's different now."

Browns fans and media were far too jaded—even at that point, before things got WAAAAY worse—to believe him. It was the sports equivalent of "You won't have Nixon to kick around anymore," pathetic, self-serving and, worst of all, not even a little true.

As it turned out, Lerner was ready to sell the team. And new ownership brings new management. Jimmy Haslam was only too happy to arrange a buyout for Holmgren. Later on, Holmgren told Peter King of *Sports Illustrated* that he regretted not taking the coaching reins himself, saying that Randy Lerner wanted him to devote his full efforts to building the team.

"Holmgren's real regret should be leaving Cleveland with $40 million in his pocket while producing no tangible results on the field," said Daryl Ruiter, who covers the Browns for 92.3 The Fan.

THE MANY MISTAKES OF RAY FARMER

It's never a good sign when a team's general manager begins a news conference with an apology to fans.

But that's exactly what Browns GM Ray Farmer did on Feb. 19, 2015, at the NFL Combine. Farmer was being investigated by the league for sending text messages to sideline personnel during games, a violation of NFL policy.

Farmer was a highly touted personnel man in Kansas City when the Browns hired him in 2013 to serve as assistant general manager under Mike Lombardi. After Lombardi was thrown over the side along with team CEO Joe Banner in 2014, Farmer became the team's general manager.

Farmer's regime didn't quite get off on the right foot after photos of him emerging from a meeting showed a whiteboard with names on it. Speculation came that the Browns' free agent targets had been revealed, but the team quickly denied it, saying it was a list of players for whom video might need to be compiled for highlights packages if a free agent signing was announced. (Bleacher Report helpfully pointed out that one of the players on the whiteboard was quarterback Rex Grossman, and "we all know there are no Rex Grossman highlights to compile.")

Farmer's first NFL Draft as GM was the one where Browns owner Jimmy Haslam opted to consult a homeless guy and draft Johnny Manziel. The other first-round pick, just as bad but nowhere near as flamboyant, was Justin Gilbert, a cornerback who washed out of the league almost as quickly as Manziel did.

It was determined that Farmer had texted to the sidelines about play calling and use of personnel. But because the texts were sharing an opinion and not designed to give the Browns a competitive edge, the punishment was not as severe as it could have been. Farmer was suspended four games, and the team was fined $250,000. Initial reports indicated the Browns might have to forfeit a draft pick, potentially in the fourth round, but that was not the case. And it's a good thing. The Browns might have been without the services of Ibraheim Campbell or Vince Mayle, the team's fourth-round picks that year.

Who, you ask? Exactly.

STRANGE INJURIES

Injuries are a part of sports. As noted baseball manager and tire dealer Lou Brown told team owner Mrs. Phelps in *Major League*, even tough guys get strains, sore arms, muscle pulls . . .

But there are some injuries that just defy belief.

LIGHTNING STRIKE AT LEAGUE PARK

On Aug. 24, 1919, pitcher Ray Caldwell came out in the top of the ninth at League Park to try and finish off his first win for the Indians.

Caldwell had already come a long way just to get to Cleveland. He'd broken into the major leagues in 1911 with the Yankees (called the Highlanders at the time). His prodigious talent led to early comparisons with Christy Mathewson, one of the best pitchers in baseball, but his skill at pitching belied an affinity for alcohol and night life.

After years of escapades in New York—trade threats, criminal charges, drying-out trips and just flat-out disappearing for days on end—he was dealt to Boston after the 1918 season. He spent less than a season there. He did all right on the mound, but his roommate was another carouser, Babe Ruth. The Red Sox wanted to keep Ruth—at least, at the time—but Caldwell was cut loose.

He'd effectively washed out of Major League Baseball when Indians player/manager Tris Speaker decided he was worth the risk, and Caldwell was signed on Aug. 19, 1919. Truth was, the Indians needed Caldwell as much as he needed them. They had finished second to the Red Sox in a shortened season in 1918, and now were trying desperately to keep pace with the league-leading White Sox.

Caldwell got Tillie Walker to pop out to shortstop Ray Chapman to start the ninth, and catcher Steve O'Neill caught a pop foul from George Burns. The afternoon sky had been getting darker, and rain started about halfway through the game but was starting to get heavier. Caldwell needed one more out, and the next batter was Joe Dugan.

Then, lightning struck, with "as much noise as the backfiring of a thousand autos or the explosion of a dozen shells from a battery of big berthas," the next day's *Plain Dealer* reported. The lightning bolt knocked off Athletics third-base coach Harry Davis' hat, and O'Neill's mask and cap. Billy Evans, one of the umpiring crew, said he felt a tingling in his legs.

Caldwell was lying on the ground on the pitcher's mound. His teammates feared he was dead. Chapman (who himself would die less than a year later from injuries sustained during a game) ran in to aid Caldwell, and nearly fell over due to numbness in his own legs.

Accounts suggested that lightning struck Caldwell on the metal button atop the cap on his head and the electricity traveled through his body before being grounded by his metal cleats in the dirt. That's theoretically possible, but unlikely. Closer to the truth is the idea that lightning struck the ground nearby—which would account for the reactions of other people on the field—or struck somewhere in the ballpark's metal superstructure (League Park was one of the first ballparks built with steel and concrete, replacing the wood firetraps that had been first used for spectators) and then traveled down to the field.

Whatever the cause, the end result was that Caldwell lay sprawled on the pitcher's mound. After five minutes, though, he came to and did what anyone else who'd just been rendered unconscious by a lightning strike would do. He demanded the ball to finish the game.

Caldwell got Dugan to ground out to end the game. And then the heavens opened up. Rain started to pour down. The win was the Indians' sixth in their previous seven games. Ultimately, they fell short of the pennant that year (to the White Sox). But in 1920, they would not be denied—due in no small part to the pitching of Ray Caldwell.

ERNIE CAMACHO'S WRITER'S CRAMP

The Indians dugout in the 1980s was full of players who were long on personality, if not necessarily talent.

Songs and stories were written about Super Joe Charboneau. Mike Hargrove acquired the descriptive but not necessarily complimentary nickname "The Human Rain Delay." And Bert Blyleven was an inveterate prankster.

And then there was Ernie Camacho, the Indians relief pitcher who was a bit flaky—and had no problem admitting it himself. "Let's just say I don't want anyone to ever think I'm predictable." he told *Plain Dealer* sports columnist Bill Livingston.

Camacho proved it one day in 1984 when he went to the training staff complaining of his pitching wrist hurting. He attributed it to overuse. He'd signed too many autographs.

Indians players were required to sign 100 autographs for charity giveaways. Most had the sense to space them out. Not so for Camacho, who, like a college student who catches up on all the reading before the finals, signed all 100 autographs in one sitting.

Fortunately, he didn't have to go on the disabled list—although one wonders what the listing might have been had it occurred. And Indians manager Pat Corrales said Camacho, who would set a team record with 23 saves that season, would remain his first call in the bullpen.

"There is only one guy who is going to get many saves with us," Corrales said, according to the *Plain Dealer*. "And that is the crazy Mexican guy in there with the bad back, sore arm and writer's cramp."

SLIDER GOES DOWN

On Oct. 14, 1995, the Indians were hosting the Mariners for Game 4 of the American League Championship Series at Jacobs Field. The Tribe trailed two games to one in the series, but had this game well in hand, with a 6-0 lead as the bottom of the fifth inning started. As Carlos Baerga came up to bat, announcers Bob Costas and Bob Uecker were talking about the recent misfortune that had befallen the Mariner Moose, who a week earlier had broken his ankle when an inline skate got caught in the turf at the Kingdome while he was skating behind an all-terrain vehicle.

Baerga laced a single to left field, but that's not what Costas was talking about.

"The umpires don't see it, but Slider is on the field," Costas announced. "The mascot had fallen out of the stands!"

It was a drizzly night in Cleveland, and Slider had been hopping around on top of the outfield wall in right field when suddenly he slipped and fell off the ledge, about eight feet, onto the warning track. Costas wondered what might have happened had Baerga's single been to right field, not left.

"I went into my somersault and instead of going head over heels, I turned over my left shoulder and could feel myself falling," Slider said in an interview published by the team for the 20th anniversary of the event. "I landed on my right leg and it completely blew up—I thought it was a compound fracture but it was a complete dislocation of my knee and every ligament tore."

Indians relievers Julian Tavarez and Jose Mesa came out of the nearby bullpen and helped tend to the wounded mascot.

"Mike Hargrove was furious in our dugout," Slider said. "And I look over at Ken Griffey Jr. [in center field] and he's cracking up."

The Indians finished off the win to tie the series at two games apiece. Game reports initially indicated that Slider would be put on the shelf for the remainder of the season, but the following night, the mascot was out on the field, albeit on crutches with his knee bandaged. Slider offered his moral support for the Indians, who were able to close out the Championship Series.

At a rally before the team's first World Series appearance in 41 years, Slider was there—using one of his crutches to play air guitar. The guy's a trooper.

ZEUS NEARLY BECOMES A CYCLOPS

When the Browns returned in 1999, nobody was happier than Orlando Brown.

Brown was originally signed by Bill Belichick and the Browns as an undrafted free agent out of South Carolina State University in 1993. He was a raw player who was ready to hit anyone—including teammates in training camp. (Belichick actually made him practice without pads while other players were wearing them, with the idea that he'd be less likely to start fights that way.)

Brown, who acquired the nickname Zeus, played three seasons with the Browns before the franchise departed for Baltimore. He was contractually obligated to play for the Ravens, but that didn't mean he liked it, even if it was closer to his hometown of Washington D.C. When he signed on with the Browns again in 1999, he told the *Plain Dealer*, "I hated the color purple! And I hated that Raven bird!"

He was expected to be a large part of the new Browns' offensive line—literally; he was 6 feet, 7 inches tall and tipped the scales at a svelte 348 pounds—and he started the Browns' first 15 games. The 1999 season's penultimate game was at home against Jacksonville. Browns center Jim Bundren was whistled for a false start by Jeff Triplette, who'd been promoted to referee earlier that year, his fourth as part of an NFL officiating crew.

The first penalty flag, thrown in 1941 in Youngstown at a college football game, was weighted with drapery weights so that it would land where intended. Since then, referees had used a variety of items to weigh down their flags, from corn kernels to sand to golf balls! Triplette's flag was weighted with BBs. In a million-to-one shot—and a stroke of extraordinarily bad luck—the flag went through Brown's face mask and struck him in the right eye.

"One minute everything was fine," Brown recalled for *Sports Illustrated* in 2003, "and the next minute—boom!—darkness, pain."

Brown said he'd originally thought Renaldo Wynn, the Jags' defensive end, had poked him in the eye before realizing he'd gotten hit with the penalty flag. Brown went off the field and then came back on, engaging with Triplette and ultimately shoving him to the ground. Brown was instantly ejected—and then taken for treatment to the Cleveland Clinic.

His ejection turned out to be fortuitous. He had swelling and blurred vision, and doctors told him there was so much internal bleeding that if he hadn't gotten to the hospital when he did, he might have lost his eye. As it was, he faced an uphill climb to get back to football.

Three days later, Brown called a news conference at which his wife read a prepared statement while he sat there wearing an eyepatch. (He wanted to read the statement but was unable to do so.) Brown was roundly excoriated and indefinitely suspended. (There was no audio of the interaction between Brown and Triplette. An NFL Films cameraman was nearby, but in a strange coincidence, he had switched off his equipment once it was revealed there was a penalty on the play—but before the flag struck Brown.)

Brown spent the 2000 season on the sideline—on the physically unable to perform list, his suspension having been rescinded once the extent of his injury was realized. The Browns released him in December of that year. He retained the attorney Johnnie

Cochran, who was still basking in the fame from serving as counsel to another football player, O. J. Simpson, and sued the league for $200 million, alleging that the flag incident prematurely ended his career. He settled for between $15 and $25 million.

Ultimately, Brown was able to return to the NFL. Despite his misgivings about wearing purple, it was with the Ravens. He played in all 16 games in 2003, a vital cog in an offensive line that blocked for Jamal Lewis in the running back's 2,000-yard rushing season. All told, Brown played in 39 more games—all with the Ravens— before he was released in 2006. He died in 2011 at the age of 40. His son, Orlando Brown Jr., is an offensive lineman in the NFL.

Triplette retired in 2018. In his last regular season game, he ejected two players—including Jarvis Landry, then with the Dolphins.

BULLETPROOF GO-GO BOOTS

Sept. 29, 2004 was supposed to be a milestone day in Kyle Denney's life. And it kind of was—even if not necessarily for the right reasons.

Denney had made his debut for the Indians earlier that month. He'd gotten his first career victory five days earlier at Jacobs Field against the Royals, and now the Indians were in Kansas City to play the Royals again. The crowd of 11,193 included several members of Denney's family, who'd driven up from his home state of Oklahoma to watch him pitch.

Denney gave up two runs in four innings pitched, ending up with a no-decision, but the Indians, propelled by a three-run sixth inning, won 5-2 to close out the series with their first road sweep of the season.

The Indians were going nowhere, and it was the end of September, so the older players had a little fun with the rookies. It was an annual tradition to make rookies wear silly costumes and parade through the airport before getting on the flight to their next destination, in this instance, Minnesota, to play the Twins in the last series of the regular season. Pitcher CC Sabathia picked out for Denney a fetching Southern California cheerleader costume, accentuated with a blonde wig and white knee-length go-go boots. (Sabathia chose the Trojans costume because at the time their football team was ranked in national polls ahead of Denney's alma mater, the University of Oklahoma.)

A *Kansas City Star* photographer captured the costume for posterity as Denney walked out of Kaufmann Stadium and onto a waiting bus. The bus pulled away, and the ballpark was still within sight when Denney recalled hearing a pop. He figured it was a firecracker, and another part of the hazing.

Then he realized his leg hurt. Then he felt blood.

"So I unzipped my go-go boot," he recalled for the *Oklahoman*— likely a sentence that has never been spoken before or since in the annals of MLB history.

As the bus had been traveling on the highway, someone with a gun had fired off a random shot. The bullet had gone through the bus, grazing teammate Ryan Ludwick before lodging in Denney's calf. Fortunately, team trainers were also on the bus, and they squeezed the muscle, popping the bullet out. Once the bus arrived at the airport, an ambulance was waiting to take Denney to a nearby hospital.

Denney changed clothes in the ambulance—the go-go boot was now officially evidence—and arrived in street clothes, disappointing hospital staff, who wanted to see the costume. His wound was cleaned and bandaged. No stitches were required. Ironically, the rookie's costume might actually have mitigated further damage: The go-go boot slowed the path of the bullet, resulting in just a flesh wound.

"I've been hurt worse getting thrown out of a barn," Denney recalled the following spring in the *Plain Dealer*.

Denney was able to face the media the following day, recovering from his wound. "I've never been so glad to have a USC thing on," he joked. However, he was ready for the media frenzy to die down, and turned down interview requests from Jay Leno, Jimmy Kimmel and *The Today Show*.

"The way he handled the situation was pretty awesome," Ludwick said, according to the Associated Press. "Now I know the guy can pitch in the big leagues, 'cause he got shot by a bullet and was about as calm as can be."

As it turned out, Denney never got the chance to pitch in the big leagues again. He spent 2005 in Buffalo, then the Tribe's Triple-A affiliate. A sprained knee after being hit by a flying bat while watching a spring training game delayed the start of his season, and he suffered a skull fracture in July after being struck by a batted ball. The Indians released him after the 2005 season. Although he latched on with the Nationals briefly, the start that ended with him getting shot after the game was his last major league appearance.

In 2016, MLB reached a collective bargaining agreement with the players union that included an anti-hazing and anti-bullying agreement. Rookies no longer would be made to wear cheerleading uniforms.

K2'S MOTORCYCLE CRASH

When the Browns drafted tight end Kellen Winslow II with the sixth overall pick in the 2004 draft, it seemed like a good move. Winslow's father and namesake was a Hall of Fame tight end with the San Diego Chargers, and the younger Winslow had received the John Mackey Award—given to the best tight end in college football—while at the University of Miami. Butch Davis, then the Browns coach and de facto personnel director, was more than willing to trade up in the draft for Winslow, a player he'd recruited but never coached for the Hurricanes.

Winslow's rookie year ended prematurely when he broke his right fibula while trying to recover an onside kick in the waning moments of the Browns' second game, against the Cowboys. The injury caused him to miss the remainder of the season.

He was ready to go for the 2005 season and had just finished minicamp when he was tooling around on a motorcycle—a sport bike he'd bought less than a month earlier. Winslow could be found riding his new Suzuki GSX-R750 through Westlake, popping wheelies through residential neighborhoods and speeding down quiet streets.

On May 1, 2005, he was riding in the parking lot of the Cuyahoga Community College west campus in Westlake. Surveillance video later showed him performing stunts across the parking lot shortly before he hit a curb and flew over the bike's handlebars, landing in bushes some 16 feet away.

Winslow was taken to the Cleveland Clinic, where he stayed for nine days for treatment of various injuries, including a lacerated liver and kidney and a torn anterior cruciate ligament that required surgery. After missing all but two games of the 2004 season, he'd miss the entire 2005 season recovering.

But his problems didn't end there. Winslow's contract—the one that made him the highest-paid tight end in the NFL—expressly forbade motorcycle riding, getting him in trouble with the team. They didn't try to recover any money from him, but by missing the entire season, he missed out on performance-oriented bonuses. And the surveillance video that found him doing wheelies and endos led to a charge of reckless operation by Westlake police.

Winslow's rookie injury had been bad luck. This time it was bad decision making—which would become a hallmark for Winslow in an NFL career that never lived up to its promise. His run-in with Westlake police wouldn't be the last experience with the criminal justice system. A series of sexual assault allegations led to Winslow pleading guilty to a rape charge and being sentenced in March 2021 to 14 years in prison.

STAPH RUNS RAMPANT IN BEREA

In March 2006, the Browns made a big splash, signing LeCharles Bentley.

The Browns were excited to sign Bentley, a productive offensive lineman for the New Orleans Saints who was listed as the top unrestricted free agent in the offseason by ESPN. And Bentley, a Cleveland native and St. Ignatius and Ohio State alumnus, was just as excited to play for his hometown team. "I can die happy now," Bentley said at his introductory press conference. "This has been my dream."

The Browns also signed Joe Jurevicius, a Lake County native whose childhood included trips to Browns training camp at Lakeland Community College

Both players would have their productive NFL careers waylaid in Cleveland, as two of six Browns players who had to be treated for staph infections in a five-year span.

Back in 2003, as the season was drawing to a close, linebacker Ben Taylor felt flu-like symptoms, but continued to come to the team's practice facility. It turned out to be staph, a bacterium that occurs naturally in most humans, but can be exceedingly harmful— and painful—when it enters the bloodstream, typically through an open cut or scrape, in Taylor's case, on his elbow. Taylor had methicillin-resistant Staphylococcus aureus, more commonly referred to as MRSA, a particularly virulent strain that can't be fought with traditional antibiotics. His temperature spiked four degrees in half an hour, and he ended up spending six days in the hospital, losing 12 pounds and undergoing surgery twice. He was able to recover, but the following season, he tore his pectoral muscle while trying to tackle the Giants' Tiki Barber, missing most of the season.

Scraped elbows turned out to be a common theme for players that ended up with staph infections. In 2005, rookie Braylon Edwards missed two games recovering from surgery to remove a skin infection from his right arm. In 2006, safety Brian Russell scraped his in an exhibition game against Buffalo, and within a few days, his elbow had swollen, and he was hospitalized, undergoing surgery to remove the infection. "I went from being in tiptop shape, to a few hours later, being knocked on my butt and having surgery," Russell said, according to the Associated Press. "It happened just like that."

Later that season, in a November game against the Steelers, Russell's incision was ripped open, and within two weeks, he had another strain of staph, ending his season. By then, the infections were piling up. After Kellen Winslow II underwent surgery to repair the ligament torn in his 2005 motorcycle crash, he developed a staph infection in his knee, requiring additional surgery and delaying his rehabilitation.

Bentley tore his patellar tendon on the first contact play at training camp in 2006. He also underwent surgery to repair the tendon, and developed MRSA. He had two staph-related surgeries, and doctors at one point contemplated amputating his leg. "At one point, I was so sick they weren't sure I was going to live through the night," he said in a 2007 interview with the Associated Press.

The Cleveland Clinic had sent a team to the Browns' practice facility in 2005 and again in 2006 to evaluate their sanitation processes, determining that the team was following proper procedures and that the incidents were unrelated. But the cases kept piling up.

In January 2008, following the Browns' best season since their return to the NFL in 1999, Jurevicius underwent arthroscopic surgery on his knee. He rehabilitated in Berea, and two weeks after surgery was reporting chills, shaking and swelling in his knee. He was also diagnosed with staph and underwent a total of six surgeries. On Oct. 9, 2008, Winslow was hospitalized with what was termed a mystery ailment. The Browns were coming off their bye with a Monday-night game looming against the defending champion Giants. Winslow spent three days in the hospital, missing the Browns' surprise win over the Giants and returning the following week, against Washington.

Following that game, Winslow and general manager Phil Savage exchanged words in the bowels of FedEx Field, and Winslow told assembled media that he'd been hospitalized for another staph infection—which he had been told by the team not to reveal—and he felt "like a piece of meat." Coach Romeo Crennel, on the hot seat as the Browns were failing to live up to expectations after winning 10 games the previous season, said Winslow's statement to the media was a distraction. Winslow was suspended for a game, but the suspension was rescinded after he produced text messages from a Browns staffer confirming his story.

"Winslow and the Browns pretended to kiss and make up," wrote *Plain Dealer* columnist Bud Shaw. "It was an air kiss."

Winslow was soon gone, dealt to Tampa Bay after the season. Also gone were Crennel and Savage. And in March 2009, Jurevicius was released as well. He then turned around and sued the Browns, alleging that unsafe sanitary practices contributed to his staph infection. Bentley filed a similar suit the following year. Jurevicius' suit was settled in 2010, and Bentley's was settled in 2012. Both were unable to leave the NFL on their own terms—and both remain active in the Cleveland area.

"These last six years have been the most trying time of my life, but now that it is over I can honestly say I am a better man for having gone through it," Bentley said in a statement released to media after the settlement was announced.

GARY BAXTER'S FREAK INJURY

As a scout with the Ravens, Phil Savage was a big fan of Baylor defensive back Gary Baxter, enough so that the Ravens drafted him with the last pick of the second round of the 2001 Draft. And when Savage moved on to become the general manager of the Browns, he wanted to bring Baxter with him.

In four seasons, Baxter had been monumentally productive for the Ravens, making 247 tackles and breaking up 36 passes, with five interceptions and two forced fumbles. He was the subject of a bidding war, ultimately won by the Browns with a $30 million contract that included a $10.5 million signing bonus. But his tenure in Cleveland was brief before a freak injury prematurely ended it.

Heralded for his durability (he'd only missed one game in college and had played 48 straight games for the Ravens), Baxter started to get injured frequently. He missed the 2005 opener with a concussion, but after that began to distinguish himself in the Browns' defensive backfield. Until his season ended in the first quarter of the fifth game of the year, against the Lions, when he tore a pectoral muscle, leading to surgery and being placed on injured reserve.

Baxter's pec continued to bother him through training camp, and he played the first two games of the season but missed the next three. He was back in the lineup against the Denver Broncos on Oct. 22, 2006, and appeared to be coming back to form, with key pass breakups and an interception.

But with less than a minute left in the first half, a backpedaling Baxter leaped to defend a pass . . . and came down clutching his left knee. He was unable to leave the field under his own power and was removed in a cart.

"It's definitely going to be frustrating and I know it's frustrating for Gary, but he's resilient and I know he'll bounce back," safety Brian Russell told the *Plain Dealer* after the game.

Baxter said the following year that he thought he'd broken both legs. "The pain was just so rough on me that I was speechless," he said, according to the *Los Angeles Times*. "When the doctors ran up to me, I couldn't say anything. I was just hollering."

But the diagnosis turned out to be grimmer—and stranger— than anyone expected. Baxter had torn the patellar tendon in each knee—the same injury that had ended LeCharles Bentley's season, and ultimately his career, in training camp. The team's signature free agent signings on defense and offense had each fallen victim to the same injury—within months of each other!

Not only had a normally injury-free player been plagued with the inability to stay healthy almost as soon as he started playing for the Browns—like the team had some kind of hex over it—but he'd fallen victim to a million-to-one injury. Baxter was believed to have been just the second player in NFL history to tear both patellar tendons on the same play.

Baxter had to spend two months in a hospital bed, but slowly, agonizingly, he rehabilitated again. Finally, in training camp 2007, he was able to participate in drills and practices. That alone was an accomplishment, but he still wanted to see the field again. However, the strength hadn't returned enough to his legs, and the Browns placed him on injured reserve on Oct. 23—a date fraught with bad memories, as it was the anniversary of his surgery the year prior and for his torn pectoral in 2005.

Baxter's contract was restructured, and he returned on a one-year free agent deal for 2008. But following another knee surgery, the Browns released him. Baxter returned to his hometown of Tyler, Texas, and became a successful businessman. He and another Tyler native who had gone on to an NFL career, Earl Campbell, started the Project Rose Research Institute for Sports Science.

"I have no screws, no pain, nothing, and I can do everything I need to do and how I need to do it," Baxter said in a 2018 interview for the Baylor Bears website. "I'm lucky."

CHRIS JOHNSON'S SPIDER BITE

On Aug. 3, 2015, the Indians and Braves made a deal that each team thought would rid them of unproductive players saddled with onerous contracts.

The Indians dealt Nick Swisher and Michael Bourn. Both had been widely heralded free agent signings prior to the 2013 season—Swisher was given what was then the largest free agent contract in Indians' history—and neither lived up to the billing. The team had won a wild card spot in 2013 but hadn't contended for a division title since. There was enough talent in the pipeline that management was willing to deal two high-priced free agents to clear the way for young prospects.

The Braves, in return, gave up Chris Johnson, who'd signed a three-year, $23.5 million extension in 2014, a little more than a year after he'd come to Atlanta in a trade from Arizona. Johnson's numbers were declining, and Braves general manager John Hart—formerly Cleveland's GM in the 1990s—was only too happy to deal him away.

It looked initially like the change of scenery did him good. In his first six games, Johnson hit .429. But on Aug. 16, 2015, while the Indians were in Minnesota, Johnson came to the ballpark with what appeared to be a bug bite on his finger. Johnson believed he'd been bitten by a spider in the team's hotel. He was treated with antiseptic and bandaged, but didn't play in that day's game (likely more due to the fact that a right-handed pitcher, Tyler Duffey, was starting for the Twins; Johnson's splits between lefties and righties were pronounced).

The next day, Johnson's entire finger had swelled up to the point where he couldn't even bend it.

"I woke up this morning and it was swollen and oozing and red. It was gross," he told reporters.

Johnson was taken to the hospital and given antibiotics. Ultimately, he spent a couple of days on the disabled list for the injury. As you might imagine, Spider-Man references were flying in the Indians clubhouse. But Johnson said if he had developed super-powers, he wouldn't spend them on a baseball diamond.

"I'll be gone," he said. "I'll be saving the world."

BEDBUGS 1, KYRIE 0

When NBA teams came to Oklahoma City to play the Thunder, they stayed at the Hilton Skirvin Hotel.

The hotel, opened in 1911 and now on the National Register

of Historic Places, was built by Bill Skirvin, an oil magnate who thought Oklahoma City needed a new luxury hotel. The 225-room palace included all the comforts of home, and was a haven for business travelers, gangsters and people generally looking for a good time.

Legend has it that Skirvin had an affair with a chambermaid, and when she became pregnant, he locked her in one of the 10th-floor rooms, from which she eventually jumped to her death. Skirvin's biographers found no evidence to corroborate the yarn, but it's been said since that the hotel is haunted, with items occasionally being moved, strange sounds being heard (some people, including writer Bill Simmons, have heard mysterious crying, like from a baby) and lights and faucets mysteriously being turned on.

Even NBA players made that claim. The Knicks blamed ghosts for a 2010 loss to the Thunder, and Tim Hardaway Jr. wrote a piece for The Players Tribune detailing the spectral activities. During a 2015 trip to Oklahoma City with the Lakers, Lou Williams refused to stay in the hotel.

But when the Cavs stayed there during a road trip in early 2016, Kyrie Irving had a different kind of scary encounter.

On Feb. 21, Irving was among the starting five for the Cavs against the Thunder, but after just nine minutes on the floor, he pulled himself from the lineup. The official story at that point was that he was experiencing flu-like symptoms. But after the Cavs' game the next day, a loss to the Pistons, Irving told the real story.

"It was honestly from the bedbugs from the friggin' Hilton that we stayed at," Irving told assembled media, lifting up his baseball cap to show several bug bites. He said he had only gotten about three hours of sleep that night.

"Just imagine how freaked out you'd be if you saw friggin' five, big-ass bedbugs just sitting on your pillow. I woke up itching, and I'm just looking around, and I'm like, 'Are you serious right now?' It was 3 a.m., and I was so tired at that point. It was, whatever."

Hotel administrators confirmed that bedbugs were found in Irving's room, but it was an isolated incident and quickly remediated. They issued a formal apology to Irving, who appeared to be none the worse for wear. The following night in Cleveland, he led the team with 30 points in a loss to the Pistons.

In 2019, Irving optioned Hardaway's Players Tribune story with a plan to make a movie about the haunted Skirvin Hotel.

TREVOR BAUER AND THE DRONE

Even before he arrived in Cleveland as part of a massive three-team trade, pitcher Trevor Bauer was considered somewhat eccentric.

He only wore one hat during his time playing for UCLA (strange even by the standards of ballplayers, normally a superstitious lot). He was fanatically devoted to unique training habits, including long tossing with weighted baseballs and the use of special tools like a shoulder tube. And his hobbies off the field included flying drones.

Bauer, infatuated with the technology after watching *Star Wars* movies, had a fleet of eight to 10 drones. The hobby was a way for him to engage with members of the general public, as he flew his drones at parks around Cleveland. And compared to players who ran the risk of injury with habits like motorcycle riding, skiing or pickup basketball, it seemed like a relatively harmless outlet.

Right until it wasn't.

In 2016, for the first time in nine years, the Indians won the American League Central Division. Their hopes for a deep playoff run had taken a hit in September when starting pitcher Carlos Carrasco took a comebacker off his hand in a game against the Tigers. His hand was broken, and he was effectively done for the postseason. A week before, another starting pitcher, Danny Salazar, who had been named to the All-Star Game earlier that season but had been struggling with injuries since the beginning of July, went on the disabled list with a shoulder strain, his season effectively over.

All of a sudden, starting pitching was at a premium for the Indians. Big things were expected of Bauer—almost by default, because there weren't a lot of starters left. He started the first game of the American League Division Series against the Red Sox, giving up three runs—all earned—in a no-decision in a game won by the Indians. The Tribe completed a three-game sweep of Boston.

In the American League Championship Series, the Tribe would meet up with the Blue Jays, who had swept the Rangers in the Division Series. Corey Kluber was on tap to start the opener of the ALCS, with Bauer following in Game 2. It would be the biggest start of his life.

Indians manager Terry Francona said that on the morning of Game 1, he got out of the shower, checked his phone, and found it was full of messages and notifications. What were they all about? "You could have given me a lot of guesses, and I wouldn't have probably got this one," he said in the news conference.

Bauer had been repairing his drone and plugged it in. For reasons even he couldn't explain, the propellers started spinning, slicing open his right pinkie finger. He needed stitches to repair it.

Francona, who was now down to what was effectively a two-man rotation with Kluber and Josh Tomlin, tried to keep his sense of humor about it, telling assembled media before Game 1, "Probably everybody in here probably at some point or another had a drone-related problem."

Bauer was pushed back to start Game 3. The day before the game, he sat down for a news conference—and brought the drone with him. "I brought my friend to answer any questions about what happened that I can't answer," he said.

An MLB rule prevents pitchers from wearing bandages on their hands, so Bauer headed to the mound with nothing but stitches, and pretty soon, the Indians were facing their worst-case scenario. Bauer faced the first four batters before Blue Jays manager John Gibbons noticed he was bleeding down his uniform and alerted umpires. "When I went to the mound and saw blood on the rubber, that's not a real good sign things are going well," Francona said during the TV broadcast of the game. Bauer was lifted from the game after throwing just 21 pitches in the first inning. But the Indians held on to win that game and eventually the series, advancing to their first World Series since 1997.

Against the Cubs in the World Series, the Indians got off to a three-games-to-one lead. The one game they lost was Bauer's start in Game 2 in Cleveland. Then Bauer pitched a potential closeout Game 5 in Chicago—and took another loss. Ultimately, the series returned to Cleveland, where the Cubs took the final two games and the series, winning Game 7 in extra innings.

Bauer went 0-2 in the World Series. Ostensibly, the injured pinkie didn't affect his grip on the ball, but you still have to wonder: Would a healthy Bauer—with all his fingers intact—have given the Indians their first World Series win since 1948?

It's a question that will bother Tribe fans until the day the team finally does bring home the title. But it didn't seem to bother Bauer. Two years later, as trade rumors swirled about him, he tweeted out that he'd cut his finger again. It was his idea of a joke.

ZACH PLESAC'S THUMB INJURY

Since being drafted by Cleveland in 2016 and making his major league debut in 2019, pitcher Zach Plesac had proven to be a dependable starter, if not one who always made good decisions. In 2020, he and teammate Mike Clevinger were told to drive home from Chicago after breaking COVID-19 protocols, and for a time both were exiled to the Indians' alternate practice site at Classic Park in Eastlake, the Lake County Captains' home field. Plesac missed four starts.

On Sunday, May 23, 2021, pitching against the Twins at Progressive Field, Plesac was perfect through three innings. And then the wheels fell off in the fourth. The Indians were leading 3-0, but Plesac gave up back-to-back hits before the Twins' Max Kepler homered to tie the game. Plesac finally got the first out of the inning, but then gave up two more runs and was lifted. Ultimately, the Indians tied the game in the bottom of the ninth, then lost it in the 10th.

After the game, Plesac was placed in the injured list. Shoulder? Elbow?

Thumb.

No doubt unhappy with his performance, Plesac was "rather aggressively taking off his undershirt," manager Terry Francona told the Associated Press, when he hit his thumb on a chair. The Indians were off to Detroit, and the next day, X-rays showed a non-displaced fracture.

Plesac did not learn his lesson after that, either. In 2022, he went on the injured list with a fracture in his pitching hand. It's uncertain precisely when the injury occurred, but the team believed it was during a game against the Mariners on Aug. 27 when, after giving up a home run to Jake Lamb, he crouched down in frustration and punched the mound, breaking his hand.

WAIT, THAT GUY WAS HERE?

Certain players are closely, even automatically, associated with Cleveland sports. It's difficult to imagine Jim Brown as anything but a Cleveland Brown. Bob Feller's entire playing career was spent with the Indians, and almost up until his death, he could be found in the press box or out as an ambassador for the team. Brad Daugherty's career, though cut short by back troubles, was played entirely with the Cavaliers, be it in Richfield or downtown Cleveland.

Some athletes and coaches were part of Cleveland at one time, although their greatest successes came elsewhere. They were here early in their careers and moved on for greener pastures, or made a stop at or near the end of the line, when their names exceeded their talents.

Some, you have a hard time remembering were ever here—but they were.

LEN DAWSON

It's a question that can sandbag all but the most hardcore Cleveland fans: Who are the two Pro Football Hall of Fame inductees who started at quarterback for the Browns?

The obvious answer is Otto Graham. He was the greatest quarterback of his era, and maybe one of the greatest of any era, his multiple accomplishments making him worthy of a statue outside FirstEnergy Stadium.

Brian Sipe and Bernie Kosar, while both beloved for their time with the Browns, don't have busts in Canton. Neither does Frank Ryan, although a case could be made. Baker Mayfield? Well, we'll see, but if the Hall beckons, it likely won't be because of his time in Cleveland.

The other Hall of Fame quarterback to play in Cleveland? Himself a Northeast Ohio native . . . Len Dawson.

Dawson was a three-sport athlete at Alliance High School and went to Purdue University, where he rewrote their record book while leading the Big Ten in passing in each of his three seasons playing.

He was taken fifth overall in the 1957 draft by the Steelers. (That turned out to be a stacked draft: The first overall pick, by the Packers, was Heisman Trophy winner and future Hall of Famer Paul Hornung. Dawson was drafted one pick before the Browns took Jim Brown. Jim Parker, another Hall of Famer, was taken 10th overall. The Browns drafted two more Hall of Famers in later rounds: offensive guard Gene Hickerson, and defensive tackle Henry Jordan, who went on to great things but in Green Bay, where he was traded two years later.)

But Dawson failed to impress Steelers head coach Buddy Parker, who instead opted to start Earl Morrall, then at the start of a lengthy career as a journeyman quarterback. Morrall became expendable—and Dawson even more so—the following season when the Steelers traded for Bobby Layne. (Layne had enough eye for talent that he told the Associated Press in 1962 that Dawson was "pro football's next great quarterback.")

Dawson was dealt to Cleveland following the 1959 season. He'd only made one start in Pittsburgh, and the road seemed just as hard for him to be a starter in Cleveland. The Browns had quarterback Milt Plum, who had been drafted in the second round in 1957.

In 1962, after Dawson had finally found success in the AFL, he told the Associated Press, "I just happened to play under two coaches who believed in sticking with one quarterback. And I wasn't that quarterback."

Dawson had one start for the Browns, coincidentally against the Steelers in Forbes Field in 1961. Plum had dislocated his thumb the week before against the Packers. The Browns got out to an early lead, but after the Steelers had come back and Dawson threw his second interception of the day, his fate was sealed.

Following the season, Dawson was released.

A former Purdue assistant who was now coaching the Dallas Texans in the upstart American Football League thought highly of Dawson. Dawson asked Browns coach Paul Brown to release him, and coach Hank Stram flew from Texas to Pittsburgh to sign him. It would be a fruitful partnership for Dawson and Stram, as the team found its footing after moving from Dallas to Kansas City. Dawson was named AFL MVP his first year in the league, and won three league titles with the Chiefs, who won the last pre-merger Super Bowl, beating the Vikings in Super Bowl IV. (The Vikings had beaten the Browns in that year's NFL championship.)

"When I think of Lenny, I think of consistency," Stram said at Dawson's 1987 induction into the Pro Football Hall of Fame. "He was always the same; he never let you see him sweat."

WALT FRAZIER

No player is more associated with the New York Knicks than Walt Frazier. He was a key part of the Knicks' championship teams in 1970 and 1973, and following his retirement from the game, is still affiliated with the Knicks, as part of the broadcast crew on MSG Networks.

But he ended his Hall of Fame playing career not in the storied venue of Madison Square Garden, but at the "Palace on the Prairie," the old Richfield Coliseum.

Frazier wasn't just a star player. In the fly-by-night NBA of the

1960s and '70s, a largely regional league with few games aired live on television, Frazier was an icon. His large two-tone Rolls-Royce could be spotted on the streets of New York, and his style demonstrated a flair all its own, with floor-length fur coats, wide-brimmed fedoras and flashy shoes.

He lived in an Upper East Side apartment with a circular bed under a mirrored ceiling, and with what he called the greatest view in the world. "When people think of New York, they think of Walt Frazier," he told the Associated Press in 1979.

Frazier was the last man standing at Madison Square Garden after those title teams. Many of his teammates had retired or moved on. And there were whispers that he was losing a step, that his reputation was more a reflection of the team around him than his own talents. There were people who believed it would be better for all involved if he'd move on.

"I guess the cool image started working against me," Frazier said in a 1977 interview with *Sports Illustrated*. "When we won, people said, "Frazier's cool, he never shows emotion.' When we lost, they said, 'Look at Frazier, he doesn't care.' The whole team changed into a group of individuals. I was the star, so I got the blame." Frazier laughed. "I was damned if I did and damned if I didn't."

Before the 1977 season began, Cavs point guard Jim Cleamons signed as a free agent with the Knicks. Cleamons had been a crucial part of the Miracle of Richfield team in 1976 and would go on to a lengthy career as a college and professional coach. NBA rules of the day dictated that the Cavaliers would get a player from the Knicks as compensation. That player was Walt Frazier.

The general reaction to this was shock. Frazier going to Cleveland, wrote Steve Hershey in *The Sporting News*, was "like putting an Eskimo in Mexico . . . like requesting Van Cliburn to play honkey-tonk at the corner pub."

But Cavs coach Bill Fitch was nothing shy of ecstatic to get Frazier. He believed Frazier could revert back to his championship form. "The worst that can happen is that Frazier will never beat me again," Fitch—famous for his one-liners—told the *Plain Dealer*.

Frazier, who said years later it felt like he'd been exiled to Siberia, hit all the right notes for his arrival in Cleveland. "This organization went out on a limb to get me," he told the *Plain Dealer*. "They couldn't afford me, but they really wanted me. How do you turn down an organization like that?"

Frazier's best year with the Cavs was his first, in which he played 59 games and averaged 16.2 points per game. The Cavs finished third in the division but made a quick exit from the playoffs—at the hands of Frazier's former team, the Knicks.

The following year, hampered by injuries, Frazier was limited to 12 games, but he remained a potent scorer, averaging more than 10 points per game. That off-season, when Fitch resigned as coach, Frazier was considered as a potential replacement. He had no plans to coach, but pointed out that Willis Reed, his former teammate, said he was similarly disinterested before being hired as Knicks coach.

Frazier appeared in three games in 1979 and then was waived. It was the end of a storied career. And the beginning of another: Frazier became part of the Knicks' broadcast crew, with his rhyming color commentaries and superlatives he said he learned reading the *New York Times* theater section.

Frazier's career in Cleveland didn't result in another championship for him—or one for the Cavs. But it was an inflection point, a moment of introspection that he says made him a better person.

"It was probably the best thing that could've happened for me," he said in a 2016 interview for NBA.com. "Because I think if I had stayed in New York, I'd probably still be 'Clyde'—running around. Now I'm in St. Croix, I'm down to earth. New York now is just a place for me to make a living."

CHUCK DALY

Just fifteen games into the 1981–82 NBA season, Don Delaney was fired as Cavs head coach. He'd been an essential part of owner Ted Stepien's front office, having been brought in—surprisingly, even to him—as general manager, and then when Stepien's first head coach, Bill Musselman, was relieved of his coaching duties (but named director of player personnel), taking his seat on the bench.

Delaney was fired as coach after a 4-11 start. Bob Kloppenburg coached three games—all losses—as interim coach while the Cavs tried to find their next head coach. They interviewed Hubie Brown, who'd turned around a mediocre Hawks team, winning coach of the year along the way. But he withdrew from consideration, essentially giving the job to the other candidate: A well-worn high school and college coach who'd been a 76ers assistant since 1978.

Chuck Daly had previously distinguished himself as a coach at the University of Pennsylvania, but now at the 76ers he knew changes were afoot, and decided it was time to move on. He actually turned down the Pistons job before latching on with the Cavs. Up until that point, Stepien's ownership had been fraught with problems and one rash move after another, but the general consensus was that the Cavs had actually made a good hire with Daly.

That the Cavs were in a precarious position in the NBA was well known to most. But Daly didn't realize how bad it was until he started his new job and found there weren't enough players to hold practice.

"I had only been there a week, and I knew I was in big trouble," he recalled in his autobiography, *Daly Life*. Sensing that he wouldn't be long for the job, he set up residence in a local Holiday Inn.

Stepien was a hands-on owner, and that wasn't a positive trait in Daly's eyes. When Daly fined a player, he had to talk to Stepien about it. Stepien wanted to talk to Daly after every game. Once, after a lengthy conversation, Daly was shocked to read the main points of it in the newspaper. He called Stepien and informed him there was a leak in the front office.

"It's me," Stepien replied. "I'm the one who told them."

Stepien's impetuousness continued to reign, with Daly saying he actually woke up each morning unsure what moves might have been made by Stepien the night before. It became clear to Daly early on that although he really wanted an NBA head coaching job, this wasn't the one.

He asked Stepien's lawyer to start drawing up separation papers. At one point, he met with Stepien at his downtown Competitor's Club restaurant. "Why don't you quit?" Stepien asked. "Why don't you fire me?" Daly replied.

The Cavs then went on a west coast road trip—and Stepien went too, to tell Daly that the Cavs' plans for the following season didn't include him.

The Cavs were now on their fourth coach in the same season—an NBA record. Stepien didn't have to look far for Daly's replacement. It was Bill Musselman again. After four coaching changes, the Cavs were right back where they started.

Daly walked away with $275,000 in severance, but still wanted a job coaching in the NBA. As it turned out, another awaited him.

"I didn't think I'd be too damaged by what happened with the Cavaliers because everyone knew how messed up they were," Daly wrote in his autobiography.

BILL LAIMBEER

One of the reasons Chuck Daly had been willing to take the Cavs head-coaching job was because he saw some talent on the roster—and that included Bill Laimbeer.

Laimbeer grew up in California (in high school, he played a Sleestak—a tall, intimidating villain—on the children's TV show *Land of the Lost* for one season) but came to the Midwest after his father, who worked for Owens-Illinois, ended up at the company's Toledo headquarters. (In those days, the NBA was not the financial juggernaut it has since become, and Laimbeer joked he was the only NBA player who made less than his father.)

Laimbeer started out at the University of Notre Dame but made a brief foray to Owens Community College to bring up his grades. He was claimed by the Cavs in the NBA draft, but an Italian team, Brescia, offered him a contract before Cleveland did. Newly married, Laimbeer and his bride spent a yearlong honeymoon in Italy before returning to the United States and signing with the Cavs.

Daly saw potential in the tall, hustling center. Laimbeer had come to camp overweight and was trying to play himself back into shape, as the backup to James Edwards. But his physical attributes and intangibles made him a beguiling trade token—and the Cavs were more than happy to cash it in, dealing him just before the deadline in 1982 for two players and two draft picks. (Of course, given Ted Stepien's propensity for trading away draft picks, they needed those badly.)

Detroit Pistons general manager Jack McCloskey also saw potential in Laimbeer and wanted him badly. Just 15 minutes before the trade deadline, the Pistons were able to swing the deal after they sweetened the pot by offering Paul Mokeski. Stepien, like Mokeski, was of Polish descent, and had a soft spot for Polish players. He wanted more white players in general, but it was for less sentimental reasons; he believed that white players would ensure more white fans.

Starting immediately for Detroit, Laimbeer made an impact right away. The following year, Daly, who'd been part of the 76ers' broadcast crew since being unceremoniously dumped by the Cavs, was hired by the Pistons, a team that was almost as moribund as the Cavs. But with players like Isiah Thomas, Joe Dumars, Dennis Rodman and Laimbeer, the Pistons turned into a dynasty, making the playoffs every year of Daly's term as coach, appearing in three NBA Finals and winning two.

The Cavs ended up getting two draft picks, including the Pistons' first-round pick, which they used on John Bagley, a serviceable player. (The Cavs had traded away their own first-round pick two years earlier to the Lakers. Because the Cavs were putrid, their original pick turned out to be the first overall, which the Lakers used to draft James Worthy.)

Edwards, the center the Cavs chose to keep over Laimbeer,

wouldn't be in Richfield for long. He was traded little more than a year later to the Suns for Jeff Cook, two draft picks and $425,000 cash. Stepien needed to make payroll.

Oh, he traded the Cavs' first-round pick in 1986, too.

LEFTY AND KNUCKSIE

Throughout their history, the Indians have been renowned for their pitching. Cy Young—the greatest pitcher in Major League history—pitched not only for the Indians, but for their National League predecessors, the Spiders. The Indians teams of the early 1950s were heralded for a starting rotation that included future Hall of Famers Early Wynn, Bob Feller and Bob Lemon. And since 2007, four different Indians pitchers have won the Cy Young Award.

And in 1987, the Indians had two 300-game winners on the roster. But that wasn't as much of an accomplishment as it sounds.

No player was associated with the Atlanta Braves in their early years like Phil Niekro. The native of the Ohio Valley made his debut with the Braves while they were still in Milwaukee, but soon was anchoring the staff in Atlanta, as an ageless, tireless knuckleballer.

"I was born a Brave, and I wanted to die a Brave," Niekro said, as recounted in the book *Game of My Life: Atlanta Braves* by Jack Wilkinson.

But the team—specifically, manager Joe Torre—had other ideas. Niekro was not-so-gently nudged out the door following the 1983 season.

Niekro still felt like he had enough left in the tank to pitch until he got at least 300 wins (at that point, he was 32 shy of the milestone). He signed with the Yankees, the oldest pitcher in an aging yet ageless rotation that included Ron Guidry and, beginning in 1985, Niekro's brother Joe. Phil Niekro won 16 games in 1984, and 16 more in 1985, with his 16th (and 300th for his career) coming on the last day of the season.

But after a decent showing in spring training in 1986, Niekro was cut by the Yankees. The Tribe quickly snagged him. He was older than the team's manager, general manager, president and most of the coaching staff.

"I'm sick of hearing I'm 47 years old," Niekro said in the *Plain Dealer*. "Somebody has to be the oldest player in baseball and somebody has to be the youngest. I just happen to be the oldest."

Brett Butler, his former teammate in Atlanta and neighbor in the offseason in Georgia, now with the Indians, sold Niekro on the team—and probably mentioned that a city like Cleveland could accommodate a polka fan like Niekro.

"It's going to be an Indian summer," Butler said in the *Plain Dealer*. "I mean, Phil Niekro's name alone is worth 10 wins. And if we can average five runs a game again, he could win 20 this year."

The Indians did score more than five runs a game, but Niekro only went 11-11. However, the team went 84-78, its best record since 1968, and expectations were high in spring training the following year (the year of the infamous *Sports Illustrated* "Indian Uprising" cover).

As the Indians were breaking camp in Arizona, they also signed Steve Carlton. It was a desperate move—and not for the Indians. Carlton, who won four Cy Young Awards between 1972 and 1982, was clinging to the game by his fingernails. The Phillies, for whom he'd had his greatest success, had released him in June 1986. He landed with the Giants, pitching there long enough to get his 4,000th strikeout before they cut him in August, and he finished out the season with the White Sox, who didn't make him an offer for 1987.

The Indians weren't in the market for a starter, but they did need another bullpen arm. Manager Pat Corrales had managed Carlton with the Phillies in 1982 and 1983, and he reached out to the lefty, who said, "I'm a starter." Corrales said they needed a reliever, and Carlton wasn't in a position to turn them down if he wanted to stay in the major leagues.

Carlton and Niekro were nicknamed "The Sunshine Boys," after the 1975 Neil Simon comedy about an aging vaudeville duo, and on

April 14, at Yankee Stadium, Niekro started and Carlton came on in relief. It was the first time one 300-game winner was relieved by another. (Rickey Henderson homered off both of them that day, for another great moment of trivia.)

Carlton made a total of 23 appearances for the Indians that season, including 14 starts. But he went 0-5 in his last seven starts before the Indians dealt him to the Minnesota Twins, who were then in the thick of a division race.

Through it all, Carlton, who always had a reputation for being standoffish with the media, remained inscrutable.

"I've never seen a more positive guy," Indians pitcher Ken Schrom told the *Plain Dealer* after Carlton was dealt. "When we got beat by Chicago 17-0 that one Sunday, I remember him saying in the bottom of the eighth inning, 'Come on, guys, all we need are two touchdowns and a field goal.'"

Not quite two weeks later, Niekro, too, was traded—to Toronto, also fighting for the East Division crown. While Carlton was no stranger to the postseason, having pitched in World Series for the Cardinals and Phillies, Niekro had spent most of his career with teams that were mediocre or worse. At any rate, he was a non-factor in Toronto, which released him at the end of August.

Carlton was left off the postseason roster for the Twins, who went on to beat the Cardinals in the World Series. But he got a ring—which he later put up for sale—and went with the team to visit President Ronald Reagan at the White House. Photo captions of the event described him as an unidentified Secret Service agent.

KEITH HERNANDEZ

As soon as free agency started in Major League Baseball, the Indians made a big splash by signing former Orioles pitcher Wayne Garland to a ten-year, $2.3 million contract prior to the 1977 season. "I'm not worth it," he told his agent, according to the *Los Angeles*

Times. And he went out and proved it, spending just five years with the Indians—and only the first one relatively healthy.

Afterward, the Indians were less inclined to dip their toe into free-agent waters—as much a reflection of ownership turmoil and tight budgets as the feeling that they'd gotten burned before.

But as the 1980s drew to a close, the Indians' fortunes were a little more secure. The Jacobs brothers had bought the team, and with their real estate fortune, cash flow was not the problem it once was. Plans were being made for a new ballpark. And the Indians scored a major coup, hiring Hank Peters to be team president and chief operating officer. Peters was a baseball lifer. He had laid the groundwork for the Athletics' dynasty of the early 1970s, and then restocked the Orioles, who won two pennants and a World Series while he was general manager.

The Indians were ready to wheel and deal, and they were in the market for a first baseman. They considered two: Right-handed Cecil Fielder, who had been tearing the cover off the ball in Japan after spending four moribund years with the Toronto Blue Jays. And lefty Keith Hernandez.

They picked Hernandez, who had won the National League MVP in 1979 with the St. Louis Cardinals before moving to the Mets in 1983.

The Mets, a laughingstock for much of their existence and always second fiddle in New York to the imperious Yankees, became the toast of the town after Hernandez's arrival, winning the 1986 World Series, and the National League East again two years later. Hernandez was a minor part of that 1988 team due to hamstring injuries, and a broken kneecap limited him to 75 games in 1989, but he still felt like he had something left in the tank. More the point, he felt he had something to prove—and thought Cleveland was the place to do it, signing a two-year, $3.5 million contract.

"Cleveland reminds me a lot of the Mets when I first went there," he told the *Plain Dealer.* "But Cleveland's pitching staff is better."

One of the reasons the Indians were willing to take a chance on him was his leadership skills.

"Keith Hernandez brings a lot of intangibles to a ballclub," Hank Peters was quoted as saying in the *Plain Dealer*. "He's a winning type of player."

But Hernandez downplayed that, saying, "A lot of the leadership thing is overplayed. Leadership is just setting an example on the field."

And that would be the problem. As the old saw goes, the best ability is availability, and Hernandez was limited to 43 games in 1990, hitting .200 with one home run in between three different trips to the disabled list due to a torn calf muscle. "It was basically a total washout of a year for him," said John Hart, the Indians' director of baseball operations and Peters' heir apparent.

The following season, Hernandez picked up right where he left off, plagued by back problems that necessitated surgery. He didn't play a game for the Indians that season but continued to collect his guaranteed paycheck—a far cry from the year before, when he said in May that he was contemplating retiring at the All-Star break because of his poor on-field performance. In what was likely damage control, Peters said as the 1991 season wound down that Hernandez's contract didn't include a buyout clause, but disability insurance helped the Indians recoup some of the cost of signing him.

At the end of the 1991 season, Hernandez was released from the 40-man roster with little fanfare, the end to what Tony Grossi, writing in the *Plain Dealer*, called "a tale of shoddy homework and flawed logic and wishful thinking."

And Cecil Fielder? All he did was hit 51 home runs for the Tigers in 1990—and then another 45 in 1991. His two-year contract cost $3 million—less than the Indians paid for Hernandez, from whom they got FAR less production. (Fielder also gets a place in Cleveland's "Wait, that guy was here?" annals, playing the last 14 games of his major league career with the Indians in 1998.)

Hernandez returned to New York for his sense of the theatric. He appeared memorably on the TV show *Seinfeld*, and since 2006 has been part of the Mets' broadcast team. He also appeared in some Just For Men commercials with another New York (and, short-term, Cleveland) sports legend: Walt Frazier.

NICK SABAN

One of Bill Belichick's first duties after being hired as Browns head coach in 1991 was to assemble a coaching staff. For a defensive coordinator, he just had to look west. On Feb. 13, Belichick announced his first hire: Nick Saban, who had just gone 9-2 in what turned out to be his only year as head coach at the University of Toledo.

Saban, a native of Fairmount, W.Va., and a Kent State University graduate, was just 39 years old. (The tandem of Belichick and Saban were such a marked change from Bud Carson and his defensive coordinator, Jim Vechiarella, that Browns executive vice president Ernie Accorsi likened it to the Kennedy administration following Eisenhower.) But Saban was already well-traveled as a coach. He'd served as an assistant for Earle Bruce at Ohio State, where he'd first crossed paths with Belichick, then a young Giants assistant scouting defensive players. From Columbus, Saban went to the U.S. Naval Academy, as an assistant to Belichick's father Steve. Saban had also served as an assistant coach at Syracuse, Michigan State and West Virginia. After being passed over when the Kent State coaching job opened, Saban went to the NFL as an assistant for the Houston Oilers—and was recruited by former Oilers coach Jerry Glanville (himself a Northwest Ohio native) to rejoin him in Atlanta.

Saban turned that job down, but he couldn't resist the Browns, saying in his introductory news conference that Northeast Ohio had the pull of home. "It was just something I couldn't pass up," he said.

Belichick and Saban had an uphill climb, having both been hired after what was then the worst season in team history, as the

Browns went 3-13. But almost immediately, the defense showed signs of improvement—and Saban suddenly became a hot commodity. He was linked to jobs every offseason, including the vacant University of Cincinnati head coaching job.

Meanwhile, the Browns defense continued to improve markedly under Saban's watch. In 1992, his second year as coordinator, the defense set five team records, including fewest touchdowns allowed (29) and most quarters without allowing a touchdown. The following year, the defense tied a team record with 48 sacks and was best in the NFL at 4.3 yards allowed per play.

And in 1994, the Browns went 11-5 and returned to the playoffs after a five-year absence, thanks in no small part to Saban's defense, which allowed the fewest points per game in the NFL that year. But the siren song of a head coaching job was too much for him to resist. He accepted the chance to succeed his mentor, George Perles, as head coach at Michigan State University.

As it turned out, he jumped ship just in time. Within a year, the Browns were headed to Baltimore, and to make a clean break from Cleveland, Belichick was fired shortly after the move was approved by NFL owners.

When promises were made for a new Browns team to take the field in 1999, new team president Carmen Policy said Saban would be a candidate worth considering—which was news to Saban, who had no type of relationship with Policy.

"I'm not concerned about or considering or thinking about or worried about any situation of any kind, anywhere, other than our team and what we're doing," Saban said in the fall of 1998.

The Browns ended up hiring Chris Palmer as head coach, and a month after the Browns won their first game, on Halloween, Saban was announced as the next coach at Louisiana State University. We all know the story from there. Saban won a national title with the Tigers, made a brief but unsuccessful foray into NFL coaching with the Dolphins and then ended up in Alabama, where he's become the greatest college football coach of all time.

DAVE WINFIELD

As the Indians moved into the new baseball-only ballpark at the corner of Carnegie and Ontario, the farm system stocked by Hank Peters and John Hart started to bear fruit. Draft picks Albert Belle, Charles Nagy, Jim Thome, and Manny Ramirez were becoming productive regular players, and the Indians were making shrewd deals, yielding Kenny Lofton, Carlos Baerga, Sandy Alomar Jr. and Omar Vizquel in trades.

As the 1994 season wore on, the Indians were in a position they hadn't seen in a generation: In the thick of a division race, with the Chicago White Sox. They needed reinforcements and turned to another aging slugger who felt like he still had a little left.

Dave Winfield was one of the preeminent athletes of the 1970s. He'd been drafted as a high schooler by the Orioles, but opted to attend the University of Minnesota, where he played baseball and basketball. He was drafted by the Atlanta Hawks of the NBA and the Utah Stars of the ABA, and although he'd never played football in high school or college, the Minnesota Vikings saw fit to spend a 17th round pick on Winfield. But the Padres picked him fourth overall, and Winfield signed with them—going to the major leagues without a day in the minors.

For all Winfield's accomplishments, the postseason had eluded him for most of his career. He played for the Padres, who were so bad that owner Ray Kroc once screamed at them over the public address system at Jack Murphy Stadium. Following the 1980 season, Winfield signed a 10-year deal with the Yankees. He saw the playoffs in 1981, as the Yankees lost the World Series to the Dodgers, but a fallow period in the Bronx soon followed. Owner George Steinbrenner blamed Winfield, whom he called "Mr. May" for his early-season performance that would fade as the year went on. Ultimately, the desire to dig up dirt on Winfield led to Steinbrenner's ban from baseball, and Winfield was only too happy to accept a trade to the Angels.

Southern California was good to him, as he earned AL Comeback Player of the Year in 1990. He finished out the 10-year contract in Anaheim and signed as a free agent with the Blue Jays, where he got what turned out to be his only World Series ring, in 1992. He then joined his hometown Twins, not far removed from a World Series win themselves.

Winfield was still with the Twins when play stopped on Aug. 12, 1994, for what turned out to be a lengthy players' strike. But as long as there was a chance that there would be baseball that year, Indians GM John Hart continued to make moves, and he acquired Winfield—while he was technically on strike—just before midnight on Aug. 31, the deadline for rosters to be set for whatever postseason might be played.

"I don't have any inside information that the strike is going to end," Hart told the *Plain Dealer* the time, "but I couldn't live with myself if we had a chance to improve and didn't do something."

Winfield waived a no-trade clause for the deal. Hart told the *Plain Dealer* that Winfield said, "I love your club and I think I can help."

Because it was during the strike, there was some confusion about terms for a guy who would be a free agent at the end of the 1994 season (an end that nobody yet realized had already happened: baseball wouldn't resume until 1995). The deal between the Indians and Twins was Winfield for "future considerations," a broader term than the cliched "player to be named later." It has entered popular lore that Hart bought Twins general manager Andy MacPhail dinner to call it square, but the truth seems to be more nebulous than that.

At any rate, Winfield was re-signed as a free agent by the Indians for the 1995 season. His biggest moment with the Indians came on Memorial Day that year, when he hit a three-run home run in a game that saw the Tribe rally from six runs down to beat the White Sox and cement their claim as the new titans of the American League Central Division.

Winfield made two trips to the disabled list that year with a rotator cuff injury. To his chagrin, he was left off the postseason roster (the Indians instead added Ruben Amaro), but he remained a bench presence, rooting on his teammates. Following the season, he hung it up. He was diplomatic as he rode off into the sunset, with nothing but warm feelings of his time in Cleveland.

"I couldn't think of a better group of guys to go out with," he told the *Plain Dealer*'s Tony Grossi the following spring. "And a better city."

JACK MORRIS

Among the new faces on the Indians' roster when they took the field for the first time at Jacobs Field in 1994 was an old hand skilled at winning, with four World Series rings.

Jack Morris was one of the most dominant pitchers in Major League Baseball—and a noted Tribe-killer, going 31-12 against mostly moribund Indians teams. In the 1980s, Morris led all MLB pitchers with 162 wins. He was the ace of the Detroit Tigers' staff when they led wire to wire on the way to winning the 1984 World Series.

In 1991, he signed with his hometown Minnesota Twins, and was a vital part of their world championship that year, starting—and finishing—a 10-inning Game 7. From there, he signed a massive free-agent contract in Toronto, using some of the proceeds to buy 7,000 acres in Great Falls, Montana, and leasing another 3,000 for a wheat farm. It would turn out to be a fateful move.

Morris led the majors with 21 wins in 1992, as the Blue Jays won the first of what turned out to be back-to-back World Series. His postseason was less than stellar, going 0-3. After going 7-12 in 1993, Morris wasn't part of the postseason roster, and following the season, the Blue Jays bought out his contract. "In my heart and mind I wasn't content walking away under those conditions," he told the *Los Angeles Times* the following year, while he was in spring training with the Indians after signing a low-risk, incentive-laden one-year "prove it" deal.

"I think they can win the World Series," Morris said after the Indians signed him. "When I left Detroit after 1990, I knew Minnesota was going to win the World Series in 1991. When I left Minnesota, I knew Toronto would win the World Series and they've won two straight. So when I say that, you should listen."

Recovering from elbow problems, Morris made $350,000 just for making the Indians' Opening Day roster. He was scheduled to start the second regular-season game at Jacobs Field—but it got snowed out, postponing his Indians debut to the next day. He got the win, then struggled for the next month, going 0-3 in his ensuing four starts. The skid inspired him to shave his trademark mustache, noting that his fortunes had reversed after doing so in 1991.

And it seemed to work, as Morris won four straight starts, including his 250th career win. Then, it started to appear that his mind was elsewhere—specifically, Great Falls, Montana, where his farm was. He would make his scheduled start and then leave for Montana to attend to matters there. He was also dealing with personal issues. An engagement was called off, and teammates claimed to have seen him in tears in the Indians dugout.

The last straw came Aug. 7, when the Indians played the Red Sox in a doubleheader at Fenway Park. The Tribe desperately needed to keep pace with the White Sox, who were leading the American League Central. They lost the first game. Morris started the second game (which was also Albert Belle's first game back following his suspension for the corked bat incident in Chicago) and let a 5-0 lead slip away. He was lifted in the fourth with a 5-4 lead and the bases loaded. "It's crunch time on the farm," he told manager Mike Hargrove, according to the *Plain Dealer* postmortem on Morris's time in Cleveland. "It's crunch time here, too!" Grover retorted.

The next batter, Tim Naehring, tied the game with a chopper over Jim Thome's head at third base.

Ultimately, the Indians rallied in 12 innings for the win, 15-10. By the time they did, Morris was gone from the clubhouse, on a plane to Montana. "That's when we decided to cut the cord," Hargrove said. Two days later—with a players' strike looming—the team announced Morris' release. He'd gone 10-6 for the Indians, who were the American League wild card team, just a game out of first in the Central, when the season ended just as abruptly as Morris' time in Cleveland earlier that week.

Morris attended spring training the following year for the Reds, but never made it to the big-league roster. His career—which was enough to eventually take him to the Hall of Fame—was over. It wasn't as ignominious an end as it would have been if he'd hung it up after the Blue Jays bought him out, but it ended on a sour note. Indians General Manager John Hart said after his release, "He can go back to doing whatever one does on a ranch."

JACK MCDOWELL

Following the loss to the Braves in 1995 World Series, the Indians identified pitching as a priority for off-season acquisitions. Their rotation was led by Orel Hershiser and Dennis Martinez, both crafty veterans, but both with more of their career behind them than ahead of them. Charlie Nagy and Mark Clark were solid starters. Ken Hill was leaving via free agency.

A premium pitcher was needed. And the Indians went out and got one, signing Jack McDowell shortly before Christmas 1995—a present, owner Dick Jacobs said, for fans.

McDowell started his major league career with the White Sox, and was a mainstay of their rotation, winning the 1993 American League Cy Young Award. But after a strike-shortened 1994 season, he was dealt to the Yankees in a cost-cutting move.

He went 15-10 in his lone season in the Bronx, leading the league for the third time in complete games, with eight. But he earned the enmity of the Bleacher Creatures for giving fans a one-fingered salute after being pulled from the second game of a doubleheader in the fourth inning as he was being shelled. McDowell apologized after the game, saying he'd lost his composure, but the damage was done. The city's tabloids called him "Jack the Flipper." The Yankees made the playoffs for the first time in 14 years, but didn't advance past the Division Series, as McDowell took the loss in Game 3 and gave up the tying and winning runs in the 11th inning of the deciding Game 5.

The Yankees didn't offer McDowell arbitration, and the Indians signed him to a two-year, $10 million deal, with a club option for a third year. It was a major coup for the Indians. McDowell had 98 wins to that point in the 1990s, more than any other pitcher that decade. Known as "Black Jack," a nickname bestowed on him by White Sox broadcaster (and former Indians player) Ken Harrelson, he brought an almost villainous intensity.

"When he was on the other team, you just didn't like Jack on general principle," Manager Mike Hargrove told the *Plain Dealer* in spring training. "It was nothing specific. It was because he beat the hell out of you. If you get your brains beat out by a guy enough, it gets personal."

The one black mark against Black Jack was his postseason record: 0-4 in two series, in 1993 with the White Sox and 1995 with the Yankees.

McDowell went a respectable 13-9 in 1996, but he called it the most disappointing year of his career to that point. The normally durable pitcher went on the disabled list for the first time in his career with a strained right forearm, and he wasn't the same pitcher when he returned.

Burdened by high expectations, the Indians won 99 games that year for their second straight division title, but it wasn't the same. The clubhouse was more tense. The nucleus that had guided the team to the best record in the majors the year before was starting to peel off. Mark Clark was traded to the Mets before the season started. Carlos Baerga was also dealt to Queens. Eddie Murray was losing at-bats and was traded to his former team, the Orioles. Albert Belle had one foot out the door as his free agency loomed.

The Indians dropped two straight to start the American League Division Series, and McDowell suddenly found himself pitching to save the team's season. It was the game they'd signed him for. He let the lead slip away thanks to a monstrous home run by B. J. Surhoff, and left a tie game in the sixth. The Indians rallied to win, but it only postponed the inevitable. They lost Game 4 to end the series and head off into a long, cold winter. (At least this time McDowell got a no-decision, instead of losses like he did in Chicago and New York.)

The following year, McDowell was moved to the bullpen early in the season—which didn't sit well with him. Then, in May, he underwent arthroscopic surgery for bits of cartilage in his elbow. He was rehabbing his way back when he was found to have a bone bruise in his arm. The Indians, who appeared to be spinning their wheels in August, shut him down for the season. The team wouldn't pick up his third-year option, bringing a quiet end to McDowell's time in Cleveland. He didn't lead the Indians to the Promised Land. He only got one postseason start, and went 16-12 in two underachieving, injury-plagued years in Cleveland. He hung on for two more years in Anaheim, but his time in Cleveland was really the beginning of the end for Black Jack McDowell.

"When you get a guy with Jack's ability," first baseman Jim Thome said in the *Plain Dealer*, "you naturally think that he could be the guy to take us over the top. It is sad and unfortunate that this had to happen."

JOHN ROCKER

After Jose Mesa's immolation in Game 7 of the 1997 World Series, the Indians cycled through several closers. Mike Jackson filled the role before leaving via free agency after the 1999 season. Then it was Steve Karsay, until at the trade deadline in 2000 the Indians dealt for Bob Wickman, a burly right-hander who attributed his sinker to the loss of a tip of his index finger in a childhood accident on the family farm.

In 2001, which was already slated to be his last year at the helm in Cleveland, General Manager John Hart had one more trick up his sleeve, trading Karsay—an impending free agent who was unhappy that he was no longer the closer—and Steve Reed to the Braves for controversial reliever John Rocker.

"With John Rocker we're bringing in a devastating left-handed late reliever," Hart said. "He's 26. A dominant closer. A workhorse who has never been on the disabled list and he has great numbers in the regular season and the postseason."

Rocker had 38 saves in 1999, and 24 more in 2000. Before the Indians acquired him, he was leading the National League in saves, with 19 in 23 opportunities for the Atlanta Braves. In more than 19 postseason innings, he had a 0.00 ERA.

But numbers tell only part of Rocker's story. His intensity (which he later admitted was steroid-aided) bordered on being unhinged. At 6 feet, 4 inches tall and 225 pounds, he looked like "10 pounds of malevolence in a five-pound bag," according to *Plain Dealer* columnist Bill Livingston. Rocker sprinted in from the bullpen for relief appearances. When fans heckled, he'd give it right back. And he had become notorious for a 1999 *Sports Illustrated* interview that had given full voice to racist, sexist, homophobic beliefs, famously denigrating riders of the New York City subway, talking about "some kid with purple hair next to some queer with AIDS right next to some dude who just got out of jail for the fourth time right next to some 20-year-old mom with kids."

As a result, Rocker was suspended and fined by Major League Baseball, an unprecedented punishment for the high crime of giving an interview to one of the most prominent and popular outlets in sports journalism.

Rocker had rubbed some teammates the wrong way too. The *Sports Illustrated* interview included him referring to teammate Randall Simon as a "fat monkey." When Chipper Jones expressed relief at Rocker's trade from Atlanta, the reliever called him "white trash." But his new Indians teammates, who were trying to get back on top of the American League Central Division after finishing second to the White Sox the year before, were willing to give him a chance—with one glaring exception.

Bob Wickman, on the verge of signing a long-term deal with the Indians, halted talks immediately. He would be OK with staying on the team for the remainder of the season as the playoffs loomed, but he, like Karsay, expected to be a closer, if not in Cleveland, then somewhere else.

It was a fraught marriage from the very start. Rocker joined the team in Kansas City, after enough flight delays and detours that he said, "I took the direct route through Oklahoma" in his introductory news conference. The Indians' next stop on their road trip was the Bronx. A reporter asked about the possible reaction he might get from Yankees fans.

"Why is reaction such a big deal to you people?" he snapped. "Who cares about reaction? The mound is still 60 feet, 6 inches away from home plate. There'll be a guy standing there with a 32-ounce bat. Who cares about reaction?"

Almost instantly, Rocker's appearance turned into a distraction. A fan in Oakland threw a beer at him while he was in the bullpen. Another, in Seattle, was wearing all white and said, "Hey, John, we've got a KKK meeting tonight and we'd like you to attend."

Rocker's time with the Indians was brief but terrible. He went 3-7 with four saves—although he was the winning pitcher for the Indians on Aug. 5, in which they came back from 12 runs down to beat the Mariners 15-14 on *Sunday Night Baseball*. Soon enough, Wickman found himself the closer again.

The Indians won their division, but were fated to play the Mariners, who'd tied a major league record with 116 wins. (The Indians were by far the weakest of the division winners, winning 91 games. Even the wild card Athletics—who couldn't play the Mariners in the first round, by rules in place at the time—had 102 wins.) Rocker made the postseason roster, but he was a non-factor on the field. In the clubhouse, on the other hand . . .

During Game 1, an Indians win, Rocker threw cups of water at heckling fans. Following Game 2, which was won by the Mariners to even the series, Rocker said, "There's a certain guy on this team who has a lawsuit filed against him for gay bashing. Why doesn't that make the papers?" The reference was to Wickman, who was being sued by a former clubhouse attendant at Yankee Stadium, who alleged that he was fired for being gay and HIV positive, and that Wickman, a Yankees pitcher at the time, had called him homophobic slurs and sexually harassed him. (The Yankees said the attendant was fired for stealing team equipment, and the lawsuit, which also named pitchers Mariano Rivera and Jeff Nelson, was eventually thrown out of court.)

After the season, Wickman was given a three-year contract—a sign of buyer's remorse by the Indians, as well as the fact that they'd move on from Rocker as soon as they could. New Indians General Manager Mark Shapiro went to the winter meetings with the intention of unloading Rocker. He didn't expect much back— he was what real estate agents would call a motivated seller—and nobody was sure he'd even find someone willing to take a chance on Rocker.

But there was one person: The same one who took a chance on him six months earlier. The Indians' succession plan had been for Hart to serve as an advisor to Shapiro after stepping down as GM, but Rangers owner Tom Hicks, no doubt impressed with the Indians of the 1990s, hired Hart, making him the highest-paid general manager in the major leagues.

"It all goes back to second chances," Hart said about his second trade for Rocker.

The Indians were going into rebuilding mode, and wouldn't win the division again for six years. Rocker made 30 appearances for the Rangers in 2002 before being released at the end of the season. He made two more appearances for Tampa the following year, and that was the end of his major league career. He's since written for far-right website WorldNetDaily and appeared on the TV show *Survivor*.

Eventually, the Indians moved on from Wickman as well—in 2006, by which time he'd become the team leader in saves (a mark later surpassed by Cody Allen).

CHRIS SPIELMAN

Even before their first practice snap after their return in 1999, the Browns had found their heart and soul—and it seemed like a match made in heaven.

Chris Spielman was an Ohio boy through and through. His father, Sonny, was an assistant coach at Massillon Washington High School, and that's where Chris and his brother Rick had played football. Spielman distinguished himself in a storied program, highly rated as a linebacker by *Parade Magazine*, Street & Smith's and *USA Today* as a senior. In fact, he became the first high school athlete to ever appear on a Wheaties box.

There was never any doubt he'd play for Ohio State—at least, not by his father. Spielman himself considered going to Michigan, but was threatened with disownment. Spielman was a two-time All-American, and ultimately was inducted into the College Football Hall of Fame for his career in Columbus.

At just six feet tall, with a 4.86 40-yard time, Spielman wasn't considered a top prospect. But Detroit drafted him in the second round. He spent eight years with the Lions, leading the team in tackles every year in what was probably its greatest span in the Super Bowl Era.

Spielman signed as a free agent with the Buffalo Bills before the 1996 season. He led the Bills in tackles that year, but the following season, had to get surgery for a broken neck, limiting his action. In 1998, his wife, Stefanie, was diagnosed with breast cancer, and the focus of Spielman's single-mindedness changed. The man who would turn the thermostat down in his hotel room to acclimate himself to cold games in Orchard Park and take stairs sideways to improve his lateral mobility stopped playing football to devote all his time to helping his wife recover. When treatment made her lose her hair, he shaved his in solidarity.

And in February 1999, the Bills were willing to send him home. They did him a favor, but it was also a good move for them. He was no longer guaranteed a starting job, and the Bills were quietly shopping him around anyway. The Browns took Spielman and the three years remaining on his contract.

"It's great to be home," Spielman said at his introductory news conference. "I was traded for a box of tape, but that doesn't bother me. I want to play for the Browns. I'm a Northeast Ohio guy, as Northeast Ohio as you can get."

He quickly became a fan favorite, due in no small part to his achievements in Massillon and Ohio State. But at 33, with a surgically fused spine, his time with the Browns was tenuous. On the first day of training camp, Spielman took a vicious hit from fullback Tarek Saleh that left him lying on the field in Berea. An MRI cleared him, and Spielman continued to play with the throttle wide open, the only way he knew how.

But in a preseason game against the Bears, he hit center Casey Wiegmann and ended up on the field, unable to move. It was a stinger, but it was also a sign. Shortly after that, he announced his playing career was over.

"For me as a northeast Ohio kid to play my last game on the Cleveland Browns field, in front of Cleveland Browns fans, in a Cleveland Browns helmet. You couldn't write it any better," he told the Associated Press.

Fans were disappointed, but they understood—and still loved him. For years afterward, Browns fans could still be spotted wearing jerseys with Spielman's name and number 54 on the back.

SHAQUILLE O'NEAL

In 2007, the Cavs made their first NBA Finals, thanks to an otherworldly performance from LeBron James in the Eastern Conference Finals against the Detroit Pistons. But there was only so much LeBron could do as the Cavs were swept by the San Antonio Spurs.

The following year, the Cavs finished second in the division and fell to the Celtics (the eventual champions) in the conference semifinals. In 2008–09, the Cavs won 66 games—a team record, but then ran up against a stacked (and, ahem, possibly chemically aided) Orlando Magic team for which the Cavs had no answers. Orlando could shoot the lights out from beyond the arc, with a 40.8 three-point percentage, and had big man Dwight Howard inside. The Cavs could only pick their poison. The Magic won the series in six games, depriving basketball fans of a LeBron James-Kobe Bryant matchup in the NBA Finals.

Clearly, a big man was needed to body up against Howard. And this looked like a job for Superman.

General Manager Danny Ferry—painfully aware from his playing days on Cavs teams that were good but not quite good enough—finally closed a deal he'd been working on even before the trade deadline, bringing Shaquille O'Neal to Cleveland from Phoenix. The Suns received Sasha Pavlovic, Ben Wallace, $500,000 in cash and a 2010 second-round draft pick. It wasn't much of a haul for Phoenix, but it would help them shed millions in payroll. (The Suns GM was one of Ferry's former teammates, in Cleveland and in San Antonio: Steve Kerr.)

Back in 1992, when O'Neal debuted in the NBA, he was not so much a player as a force of nature. He rapped. He acted. He referred to himself as "The Big Aristotle." But on the court, he backed it all up. He had been player of the year while in college at Louisiana State University and was NBA Rookie of the Year with the Magic. He won three titles with the Lakers—being named the Finals MVP each time—and another with the Miami Heat.

So unsurprisingly, his arrival in Cleveland brought with it a flurry of jersey and season-ticket sales. Even though he was 37, people still wanted to see him.

In 2008, the year before he came to Cleveland, he had been an all-star with the Suns, as the nomadic end portion of his career was starting. But he knew his role in Cleveland.

"My motto is simple," O'Neal said, according to the Associated Press. "Win a ring for the King."

Both LeBron and Shaq would be free agents after the season, but Shaq left open the possibility of signing an extension in Cleveland—and suggested LeBron could have every reason to do the same. "If we do what we came here to do, everything will fall into place," he said.

He knew he wasn't the star of the team, and he was OK with that. But after an all-star season in Phoenix's uptempo game, big things were expected from Shaq with a half-court offense that more suited his skill set. It seemed like he made a good pairing with Zydrunas Ilgauskas, the team's other big man.

But Shaq missed the last six weeks of the season with torn thumb ligaments, playing in only 53 games. Even without him, the Cavs blew through the regular season, winning 61 games, five fewer than the year before but still tops in the NBA that year. After dispatching the Bulls in the first round of the playoffs, the Cavs faced the Boston Celtics, ultimately losing in six games—as it turned out, the last six games of LeBron James' tenure with the Cavs (at least, the first time).

Six weeks later, LeBron was on television from Connecticut, proclaiming that he was headed to Shaq's old stomping grounds of Miami. Shaq left town too—for Boston, where his playing career, one that had been filled with illustrious moments, ended not with a bang, but with a whimper.

KYLE SHANAHAN

The Browns since 1999 have had a steady stream of coaches whose brilliance fell short of their reputation.

Butch Davis? Well, we've already gone over that. Romeo Crennel had one good year as Browns head coach. Problem was that he coached in Cleveland for four years. Eric Mangini never lived up to his reputation as the Mangenius.

But one assistant coach got the most that he could out of the Browns offense—and then got the hell out of town after one year: Kyle Shanahan.

Rob Chudzinski, who grew up a Browns fan in Northwest Ohio and served as an assistant to Davis and Crennel in Cleveland, was thrown over the side in 2013 after one 4-12 season as head coach. A frenzied and haphazard search for a new coach—after prospective deals with Jim Harbaugh and Josh McDaniel fell through—yielded Mike Pettine, who had served as a defensive coordinator in Baltimore and Buffalo.

Pettine, looking for an offensive mind to call plays, turned his sights to Kyle Shanahan, who was newly unemployed. He had served as offensive coordinator for his father Mike Shanahan in Washington. But when owner Dan Snyder was forced to choose between Robert Griffin III, the quarterback he mortgaged the farm to draft, and the coaching staff, he kept Griffin and fired Shanahan and all his staff.

Shanahan senior—the man who'd gotten John Elway a pair of rings after nothing but lopsided losses in the Super Bowl—was heralded as an offensive mastermind. Kyle, on the other hand, still hadn't shaken the reputation as a nepotism hire, working as an NFL assistant for his father—or his father's friend, Gary Kubiak.

The Browns saw something in Kyle Shanahan (who had already been turned down for offensive coordinator positions in Miami and Baltimore) and picked him up off the discard pile. Even Griffin was magnanimous when asked about him, saying, "I think Kyle has a great, innovative mind and does some great things with the play calling and formations. Nobody can ever knock him for that."

The Browns then drafted Johnny Manziel, sowing the seeds for another shotgun marriage with a putative franchise quarterback. But the starting quarterback for the Browns would be Brian Hoyer, who had taken the reins the year before and even distinguished himself before tearing his ACL on a Thursday night game against the Bills. The Browns' stout offensive line and run game allowed Hoyer to blossom in Shanahan's read-option system, succeeding with bootleg runs and play options.

In November of that year, the Browns were 6-3 and leading the AFC North. And then the wheels fell off. Center Alex Mack broke his leg in a decisive win over the Steelers, and the zone blocking started to falter. The Browns started losing, and fans—and some higher-ups in the Browns organization—started clamoring for Manziel to start (this was the season that saw general manager Ray Farmer texting to the sidelines on just that topic). Finally, after a 25-24 loss to the Colts in a game that saw two Browns defensive scores, Hoyer's position as starter had become untenable.

Manziel started the following week, a home game against the Bengals that the Browns needed to win to stay in the playoff hunt. The Browns were drubbed 30-0. Manziel threw for 80 yards—and two interceptions, matching Hoyer's total from the week before. What seemed like a clear-cut situation had finally become very murky.

After four years in Washington, Kyle Shanahan could recognize a dysfunctional organization. And the Browns definitely qualified. He'd signed a three-year contract but had no urge to stay. Shanahan laid out a 32-point case in a document (NOT a PowerPoint, he clarified several years later) why he should be let go, and Pettine was willing to comply, saying later that holding Shanahan to his contract when he didn't want to be there wouldn't have been good for anyone.

As it turned out, letting him go didn't help anyone in Berea, either. The Browns went 3-13 that year, and Pettine, along with

Farmer, was fired after the season. Manziel had been given the chance to start and he became more notable for his partying and police interactions than actually accomplishing anything on a football field. As soon as the new NFL year began the following March, he followed Pettine and Farmer out the door.

And Shanahan? He ended up as the offensive coordinator in Atlanta. In his second year with the Falcons, they advanced to the Super Bowl, and at one point led the Patriots by 25 points. The bad news was that one point was not the end of the game. Thanks in no small part to Shanahan's conservative offensive play calling in the second half, the Patriots mounted the largest comeback in Super Bowl history, winning in overtime.

The day after that crushing loss, Shanahan was announced as the new head coach of the San Francisco 49ers. It would take three years, but he would take that storied franchise back to the Super Bowl . . . and blow a lead to the Chiefs. That one was only 10 points.

ANDREW BOGUT

If you ask Golden State Warriors fans, Andrew Bogut's absence is what made the difference when the Cavs rallied from a 3-1 deficit to win the 2016 Finals. (But they're not as willing to engage in the thought exercise that Kyrie Irving's injury in the 2015 Finals made the difference in the Warriors' favor.)

Bogut missed the final two games of the 2016 Finals after injuring his left knee in Game 5. The Cavs won both games, giving the Cleveland its first major sports championship since 1964. Then in the offseason, the Warriors signed Kevin Durant, making Bogut both expendable and too expensive to keep. He was dealt to the Dallas Mavericks, starting a veritable carousel of stops for the big man, who had been drafted first overall in 2005.

Bogut missed a total of 17 games with the Mavericks due to various injuries, and in February 2017 was sent to Philadelphia as part of a trade. The 76ers waved him, and he had his pick of several teams who were pursuing him.

He chose Cleveland, telling NBA reporter David Aldridge, "I heard it's beautiful this time of year."

More seriously, he turned down bigger contracts with the opportunity of more playing time for the chance to win a title with Cleveland. It was planned that he'd get some key minutes, since at that point, Kevin Love was recovering from knee surgery. As it turned out, Bogut got less than one minute of playing time in a Cleveland uniform.

He made his debut with the Cavs against the Heat on March 6, 2017, getting a huge ovation when he checked into the game for the first time, near the end of the first period. But with 11:38 remaining in the second, he banged knees with Okaro White, whom he was guarding around the three-point arc. Bogut went down immediately, clutching his left leg—the same one he'd injured in the 2016 Finals. Teammates James Jones and Tristan Thompson helped Bogut, who couldn't leave the court on his own power, to the locker room. He'd broken his tibia—the larger of the two bones of the lower leg—confirming the diagnosis of everyone who'd heard it in the building and on TV. "I heard it break," LeBron James said after the game.

The Cavs waived Bogut a week after his injury, eating an estimated $1 million in cap space. As it turned out, the Cavs advanced to their third straight Finals—where they lost to Durant and the Warriors. But not with Andrew Bogut, whose entire Cavs career took 58 seconds of game time.

"He didn't even get a minute," James said.

DWYANE WADE

As highly touted picks in the 2003 Draft, LeBron James, who went first overall, and Dwyane Wade, taken fifth by the Heat, would always be linked. Beyond that, they were close friends, playing together on the U.S. Olympic team and then, starting in 2010, with the Heat. But LeBron returned to Cleveland after four years, while Wade stayed in Miami.

Wade and the Heat weren't able to come to an agreement following the 2015–16 season, and Wade departed, somewhat acrimoniously. He signed a two-year contract with his hometown Chicago Bulls, but after the first year, he was bought out.

A free agent, Wade drew interest from multiple teams. But he ended up in Cleveland, largely at the behest of his buddy LeBron, who was delighted by the signing. "It's kind of like when you start school," LeBron told the Associated Press, "and you walk into the classroom and you're not quite sure who your classmates are and when you walk in there and one of your best friends is in there, you're like, 'Oh, yeah, this is going to be fun. It's going to be a good class.' That's the type of feeling I got."

Less enthused was J.R. Smith, who would be displaced for Wade to make the starting lineup—at least initially. But after three games—in which he shot 7-of-25 from the floor—Wade would no longer be in the starting lineup. Cavs' head coach Tyronn Lue said it was Wade's idea.

For a while, the arrangement seemed to work. James touted his friend as a potential sixth man of the year as Wade came off the bench for a stretch that saw the Cavs go 18-1. But there was another new piece of the puzzle. The previous summer, the Cavs had dealt Kyrie Irving to Boston for point guard Isaiah Thomas. But Thomas had a hip injury that appeared worse than initially reported (enough that Boston threw in an extra draft pick to complete the trade to Cleveland) and didn't make his debut with the Cavs until after the new year. It was not an easy integration, and the Cavs struggled.

Thomas was traded at the deadline to the Lakers as the Cavs overhauled their roster. Also dealt was Wade, who returned to the Heat.

"I mean, I hated to see him go," James told ESPN, "but, I mean, listen, I felt like that's where he belongs."

"It just wasn't working," Wade said in an interview with ESPN following the trade. "It just wasn't fitting the way a championship organization want to see fit . . . Guys are happy and I don't want anyone to talk bad about the guys that [were] there like it was their fault. It didn't work and everyone's moved on to their respective places and everyone's happy."

Ultimately, the overhaul on the Cavs roster worked. Entering the playoffs as a four seed, the Cavs were able to advance to their fourth-straight NBA Finals (which they lost in a sweep by the Warriors). And Wade mended fences with Heat management, even signing a one-year extension for a farewell tour.

And if nothing else, Wade can laugh now about his 46-game stint in Cleveland. It wasn't long before the Cavs got another D-Wade. While Dean Wade was playing a game early in 2021, Dwyane Wade tweeted, "I hope he has a better Cleveland career than I did." Responses from Heat fans indicated they refused to believe he ever played in Cleveland, while Cleveland fans will still occasionally refer to "Cavs legend Dwyane Wade."

JOHN BEILEIN

Dan Gilbert owns the Cleveland Cavaliers, but his Michigan roots run deep. He grew up in the Detroit area and attended Michigan State University. Quicken Loans, the company he founded that made him wealthy, is headquartered in Detroit, and his substantial real estate holdings in Cleveland are dwarfed by the properties he owns in Detroit.

That Michigan influence bled into his Cavs ownership. One of the first things he did following his purchase of the team was bring Detroit Pistons announcer Fred McLeod to Cleveland. (The move was met with resistance, but McLeod became an essential and beloved part of Cavs fandom until his premature death in 2019.) Gilbert made repeated entreaties to various Michigan sports icons to come to town. He tried to hire Michigan State coach Tom Izzo in 2010 as an inducement for LeBron James to stay in Cleveland. (No doubt Izzo would have moved to Strongsville, near the home that Bill Cowher supposedly would buy whenever rumors surfaced that the Browns were on the verge of hiring him). In 2017, the Cavs pursued Chauncey Billups, a former five-time all-star and Finals MVP with the Pistons, to be their general manager. Neither move panned out.

Gilbert finally landed his Michigan man when John Beilein was announced as the Cavs' new coach in 2019. Beilein had no NBA coaching experience, but success had followed him wherever he went—and the 66-year-old had no reason to believe it would be any different with the Cavs. He'd spent 12 years at the University of Michigan, becoming the winningest coach in the school's lengthy history. Prior to coming to Ann Arbor, he'd rebuilt programs at Canisius, Richmond and West Virginia, developing quality high school players into potential NBA Draft picks. He was heralded as just the kind of coach the Cavs would need as the team returned to respectability after LeBron James' departure.

"I looked at this job and said, 'This feels just like the Michigan opportunity,'" Beilein said in his introductory news conference. "People say, 'You're crazy. Why are you changing these jobs and doing something different?' It just felt like this was a healthy change ... and an opportunity to do something else."

Beilein was given a five-year deal, but he knew Gilbert had a quick trigger finger for firing coaches. He'd be the sixth head coach since the Cavs fired Mike Brown in 2010. But that didn't bother him. "I never gave it one single thought, not in any way," Beilein said.

He probably should have. Beilein didn't even last an entire season with the Cavs—easily the shortest tenured coach in the history of Dan Gilbert's ownership. In fact, his 54 games were second only to Chuck Daly for non-interim Cavs coaches.

In his introductory news conference, Beilein eschewed the use of the word "rebuild," saying the Cavs would go through a "renaissance." But the team ended its preseason with two lopsided losses to the Celtics, leaving Beilein to wonder what he was really in for.

In December 2019, a report surfaced in The Athletic, with Cavs players—anonymously—saying that they'd tuned out Beilein, who appeared to be treating them like he did any other college athlete he'd worked with.

The following month, Beilein made a public apology for a film session in which he said the team was playing like a bunch of thugs. (He said he meant to say slugs.) And all the while, the Cavs kept losing, assembling separate skids of six, seven and eight games during what was shaping up to be a forgettable season. Andre Drummond, who was traded to the Cavs by the Pistons, said the situation he found in Cleveland was worse than the one he'd left. And the Cavs didn't appear to be showing any kind of growth, with a better roster looking just as bad as the first post-LeBron team the season before.

Finally, after the All-Star break, Beilein and the Cavs parted ways. J.B. Bickerstaff, who'd interviewed for the head coaching job before Beilein was hired, and was hired as one of Beilein's assistants, succeeded him as head coach. The agreement meant the now ex-Cavs coach would be paid for the entirety of the season (which itself would end abruptly for the Cavs a month later as COVID-19 forced a shutdown) but would forgo $12 million in guaranteed money over the next four years.

He wanted out that badly.

ODELL BECKHAM JR.

Like Walt Frazier a generation earlier, Odell Beckham Jr. was more than just an athlete in New York. He was an icon. His sense of style was just as pronounced—and just as popular—as Clyde's, although his resume was a little thinner.

Beckham was recognized as a talented receiver with the Giants, but quarterback Eli Manning's time with the team was running short, and it looked like a complete rebuild was at hand. There were also whispers that Beckham was a distraction and even then, although he was a dynamic playmaker, he had a hard time staying healthy.

The Browns, following a pleasantly surprising 2018 season, traded for Beckham, sending draft picks and Jabrill Peppers to the Giants. Reaction was hyperbolic in Cleveland. It was the move that would put the Browns over the top.

Beckham took the deal personally. "They thought they'd send me here to die," he told *Sports Illustrated*.

But by all accounts, he was a good teammate. Like Frazier, he got a new, instantly recognizable Rolls-Royce, an orange sport-utility vehicle, with a custom hood ornament of him making that one-handed catch on *Sunday Night Football*. His first year in Cleveland, he played all 16 games, catching 74 passes for 1,035 yards—despite a sports hernia and the Browns' offensive woes in a 6-10 season.

The following year, Beckham was limited to seven games after tearing his ACL against the Bengals. He missed the majority of the Browns' 11-win season—the most since they'd returned in 1999—and their first playoff win since Bill Belichick coached the team.

Beckham was determined to come back in 2021. As it turns out, he was also determined to leave Cleveland.

On the morning of the NFL trade deadline, Nov. 2, 2021, Beckham's father, Odell Beckham Sr., shared a video on social media. Set to the R.E.M. song "Everybody Hurts," it showed multiple occasions where Beckham was open but quarterback Baker Mayfield was unable or unwilling to pass the ball to him.

Later that day, LeBron James sent a tweet about Beckham that included the hashtag #FreeOBJ. Beckham didn't publicly address either social media posting and was ready to come to practice in Berea the following day, where other players and staff felt blindsided. "There's not a manual for this one," Mayfield said, according to CBSsports.com.

Beckham got his wish and was cut loose Nov. 5. It was estimated that he left millions on the table when he signed with the Los Angeles Rams a week later. Stories started to get out that Southern California had been his destination all along.

It was a strange end, but it seemed the inevitable one. Stories had surfaced as early as 2019 that Beckham wanted out of Cleveland, and was yelling "Come get me" to opposing players. After that season, Beckham joked about those rumors with the media, saying that he'd talked to a couple of Canadian Football League teams about possible trades, before quickly adding, "I'm not going anywhere. We'll figure it out. It's just too special to leave."

Apparently, it wasn't.

REFERENCES

NEWSPAPERS

The Atlanta Constitution
The Baltimore Sun
The Boston Globe
The Boston Herald
The Buffalo News
The Canton Repository
The Cleveland Plain Dealer
The Chicago Sun-Times
The Chicago Tribune
The Dallas Morning News
The Hartford Courant
The Lorain Morning Journal
The New York Daily News
The New York Times
The Oklahoman
The Pittsburgh Post-Gazette
The Pittsburgh Tribune-Review
The Richmond Times-Dispatch
South Florida Sun-Sentinel
The Tampa Bay Times
USA Today
The Washington Post

MAGAZINES

Forbes   Sports Illustrated

WEBSITES

Bleacherreport.com   NFL.com
Deadspin.com   Profootballtalk.com
Espn.com   Sabr.org
Grantland.com

BOOKS

Daly, Chuck, *Daly Life: Every Step a Struggle*, High Top Publishing, 1993

Gitlin, Marty, *The Cleveland Cavaliers*, Sportzone, 2011

Halberstam, David, *The Education of a Coach*, Hachette Books, 2006

Livingston, Bill, *George Steinbrenner's Pipe Dream: The ABL Champion Cleveland Pipers*, Kent State University Press, 2015

Pluto, Terry, *The Curse of Rocky Colavito*, Gray & Co. Publishers, 1994

Schneider, Russell, T*he Cleveland Indians Encyclopedia*, Sports Publishing, 2004

Sommer, Mark, *Rocky Colavito: Cleveland's Iconic Slugger*, McFarland Publishing, 2019

Sulecki, Jim, *The Cleveland Rams: The NFL Champs Who Left Too Soon, 1936–1945*, McFarland Publishing, 2016

Torry, Jack, *Endless Summers: The Fall and Rise of the Cleveland Indians*, Taylor Trade Publishing, 1996

ACKNOWLEDGEMENTS

As is the case with all great works of literature, this book began with a conversation on Twitter. Noted social media bomb-thrower Chris McNeil started talking at length about bizarre moments in Cleveland sports history. His voluminous following started contributing their own, and I said, "You know, this isn't a bad book idea." Chris encouraged it, and before I knew it, I had an outline. I talked Chris into a parade. He talked me into a book. So I think we're even at this point.

Growing up in Youngstown in the 1980s, I could have just as easily been a Pittsburgh fan (although my father's a Bengals fan, and there was a small but vocal pocket of 49ers fans too). Bernie Kosar tipped the scales in Cleveland's favor for me, so this book is his fault.

Thanks to David Gray, copy editor Frank Lewis and everyone at Gray & Company Publishers for making this project a reality as well. Each book is its own experience, and David was happy and helpful, guiding me along the way.

I will match my sports trivia knowledge up against anyone else's, but even I had to do research. I have a small cadre of friends and well-wishers who assisted me in this effort, including, but not limited to, Bill Barrow and Vern Morrison, now retired from Cleveland State University (I'm told that by mentioning Vern's name, I'm guaranteeing that he'll buy my book), and John Skrtic and Brian Meggitt at the Cleveland Public Library. I'm a member of SABR, which opened up a whole new world of people and research resources. If you're a baseball fan, please consider joining.

Ryan Crincic—whose sports knowledge dwarfs my own—took an early look at the outline, and Zach Baker read early drafts.

Both offered helpful notes and corrections that will make me look slightly less ridiculous than I actually am.

Writing is a solitary pursuit. But I've been fortunate enough to have a small army of friends and well-wishers, from my current colleagues at the Chronicle-Telegram to my former Gannett co-workers, including Kristina Smith, Chad Conant and Daniel Carson. My fellow travelers in the writing community are numerous and wonderful, starting with my friend and mentor, the Rev. Dr. Joe Boyle, and including Jim Vickers, Colleen Smitek and Dillon Stewart at Great Lakes Publishing, Ryan Schnurr at Belt, Stephanie Liscio, Steve Halvonik, Will Harris, Dom Zuccone (who is a member of my tribe in both the biological and vocational sense), my social media hype man Rich Kocemba, and Pete Croatto and Luke Epplin (both of whom mentioned me in their recent works, so I feel obligated to return the favor).

And of course, I have a lot of family in my corner. My parents, Chuck and Rose, are two of my biggest fans, and Tony and Linda, my in-laws—both Yinzers—will nonetheless tout this book because I wrote it. I also rely on the support—technical and otherwise—of my brother Adam (who always gets upset when I don't mention him). Last but by no means least, I'd like to thank my wife Shannon and my daughter, to whom this book is dedicated. I promise I'll have more spare time now . . . at least until the next project.